MW00622793

PRAISE FOR
WELCOME TO THE BASEMENT

"When did we become so accustomed to the world around us that we forgot to live by the world within us? The world that reflects the Creator we serve? The life that doesn't fit in but stands out? This book will inspire you to stop blending and start standing. Allow the Holy Spirit to transform you from the inside out, and soon you will find yourself turning the world upside down."

—CHARLOTTE GAMBILL, BESTSELLING AUTHOR,
SPEAKER, AND LEAD PASTOR OF LIFE CHURCH

"Tim Ross is a contemporary incarnation and exciting example of God's truth! His mission and ministry seem to follow none of the traditional rules and roads to fulfilling the call of God. In *Welcome to the Basement* Ross reveals the struggle on the pathway climbing down from the mountaintop—or rather the rooftop—of success to basement blessings. Prepare to tour the back stairs 'down to the basement' of the center of God's will."

—KENNETH C. ULMER, DMIN, PHD, SENIOR
ADVISOR ON COMMUNITY RECONCILIATION TO
THE PRESIDENT OF BIOLA UNIVERSITY

"Tim Ross brings depth and authenticity to everything he does because it's who he is. His ability to unpack Scripture and connect revelation to everyday life is transformational. Your heart will be touched, your head lifted, and your heart stirred by his bold declaration of the gospel."

—RICH WILKERSON JR., LEAD PASTOR AT VOUS CHURCH

"Witnessing Tim's level of consistency over the last two decades has been astonishing. His faithfulness to God and family in tandem with a knowledge of theology shine a light not only to people of the church but also to those outside the church. As you read *Welcome to the Basement*, you will be elevated to another level of knowing God, knowing your purpose, and knowing your assignment. You will learn that the way up is down—down to the Basement, a place of humility and vulnerability—before you reach a place of elevation."

—JEROME LEWIS, SENIOR PASTOR AT
SEEDS OF GREATNESS CHURCH

"Tim Ross embodies the seemingly paradoxical combination of authentic gentleness toward people and fierce revolutionary passion toward making a difference. This book will inspire readers to see that gentleness and passion aren't optional extremes to choose between; instead, they are the necessary ingredients to trigger the real change our world desperately needs."

—MARK VARUGHESE, SENIOR LEADER OF KINGDOMCITY

"Every time we interact with someone, we make an impression on them. It's easy to get so caught up in the details of our busy schedules that we forget that we are called to share the love of Jesus with every person we come in contact with. In *Welcome to the Basement* Tim Ross gives us a beautiful picture of how we can turn someone's life upside down by showing them who Jesus is. For as long as I've known Tim I've admired his heart for all people and his passion to share the message of love and hope that Jesus brings. This book will give you practical ways to be a light to all those around you. I'm so excited for you to get your hands on this book, and I know you'll be blessed as you read *Welcome to the Basement*."

—CHRIS DURSO, BESTSELLING AUTHOR AND SPEAKER

"Authors are everywhere, but voices are extremely rare. Tim Ross is an essential voice perfectly positioned for the day in which we live. And this book? Let's just say your neighbors, friends, and family who don't yet know Jesus will thank you for reading it. *Welcome to the Basement* is guaranteed to change the way you walk out your walk with Christ."

—PRESTON MORRISON, SENIOR PASTOR OF PILLAR CHURCH

Welcome to the Basement

AN UPSIDE-DOWN GUIDE TO GREATNESS

TIM ROSS

NELSON
BOOKS

An Imprint of Thomas Nelson

Published in Nashville, Tennessee, by Nelson Books, an imprint of Thomas Nelson. Nelson Books and Thomas Nelson are registered trademarks of HarperCollins Christian Publishing, Inc.

Thomas Nelson titles may be purchased in bulk for educational, business, fundraising, or sales promotional use. For information, please email SpecialMarkets@ ThomasNelson.com.

Unless otherwise noted, Scripture quotations are taken from the Holy Bible, New Living Translation. © 1996, 2004, 2015 by Tyndale House Foundation. Used by permission of Tyndale House Publishers, Inc., Carol Stream, Illinois 60188. All rights reserved.

Scripture quotations marked ESV are taken from the ESV® Bible (The Holy Bible, English Standard Version®). Copyright © 2001 by Crossway, a publishing ministry of Good News Publishers. Used by permission. All rights reserved.

Scripture quotations marked NIV are taken from the Holy Bible, New International Version®, NIV®. Copyright © 1973, 1978, 1984, 2011 by Biblica, Inc.® Used by permission of Zondervan. All rights reserved worldwide. www.zondervan.com. The "NIV" and "New International Version" are trademarks registered in the United States Patent and Trademark Office by Biblica, Inc.®

All emphasis in Scripture quotations is added by the author.

Any internet addresses, phone numbers, or company or product information printed in this book are offered as a resource and are not intended in any way to be or to imply an endorsement by Thomas Nelson, nor does Thomas Nelson vouch for the existence, content, or services of these sites, phone numbers, companies, or products beyond the life of this book.

ISBN 978-1-4002-4777-6 (ePub)
ISBN 978-1-4002-4778-3 (HC)

Library of Congress Control Number: 2023946584

Printed in the United States of America
23 24 25 26 27 LBC 5 4 3 2 1

To Jesus, thank You for turning my life upside down.
To Juliette, thank you for believing in me. You're
my favorite person in the whole world.
To Korey, thank you for friendship. We
are the first two Dwellers for sure!
To Preston, thank you for twinship. May the editors
stay mad that they can't change this word I made up.
To Charles and Maxinne Ross, thank you for
being my parents, pastors, and praisers.
To Nathan and Noah, thank you for allowing me to
be your father now so that we can be friends later. I
hope the best of me is carried out in the two of you.
To the readers, thank you for pressing B. It
wouldn't be the same down here without you!

I love you,
Timothy

CONTENTS

CONTENTS

PART THREE: IDENTIFYING UPSETTERS

PART FOUR: DISTURBING THE PIECE

PART FIVE: FITTING IT ALL TOGETHER

FOREWORD

by Michael Todd

*I*t was one call. One call changed my life. One call from another continent. On a Saturday morning when I was about to give up the ministry, I got a call from Tim Ross. From Australia. And he said that the Holy Spirit had laid me on his heart.

What he didn't know was that day I was contemplating giving up on ministry. But he was sensitive enough to call a no-name youth pastor who had met him one time. And as I paced around in my backyard, he ended up counseling me that day to not give up on ministry. When he got back to the US three days later, he invited me to his home so he could sit down at a dining room table and introduce me to the concept of the Basement.

For three days he walked me through Scripture, walked me through metaphors, walked me through basketball analogies, walked me through video game analogies, trying to unlock the mystery of God's kingdom and help me understand what it is to live HOT. He says this stands for Honest, Open and Transparent. I say Humble, Open, and Transparent, which is all the same thing:

to live a life that deals with what's real but always puts that life up against the light of the Word of God.

I would not be the man I am today, I would not have reached as many people as God has allowed me to reach today, and I would not be the husband and father that I am today had I not pressed B for the Basement over a decade ago.

Before there was a podcast, before I was a lead pastor, before *Relationship Goals*, before *Crazy Faith*, before *Damaged but Not Destroyed*, before Embassy City Church, before I had enough money to buy a coach plane ticket, Tim Ross sat down at a dining-room table and introduced me to the concepts that are in this book. I'm telling you that the message, the methods, and the principles that you are about to read have the power to change the trajectory of your life.

I didn't know that going down would be the thing that allowed God to lift me up. And I'm so excited for you because if you picked up this book, you have the opportunity to do more than you ever thought was possible. Because this is not just a good idea from Tim Ross. This is God's playbook on how to use His children in a way that affects the world.

I love you, Tim. Thank you for inviting me to the Basement so we can represent and upset the world.

INTRODUCTION

Get Down Here: An Invitation to the Basement

*I*f you're coming to this book from *The Basement* podcast, welcome! It's hug time! We're about to go deep just like we do on the podcast.

If you're coming here from my last book, *Upset the World*, thank you so much for your support! I love you! I want to give you a little context before you embark into the following pages.

Here's the thing: at the time I worked on *Upset the World*, I didn't know God was going to give me the context I'm about to give you. Without that context, you can just frisbee that book. Pulp it. Make it a coaster.

If you haven't read it yet, don't worry about it. Don't look for it—you can't get it. It's out of print on purpose.

I stand by everything I said in those pages—some of the overarching themes here might even sound a little familiar—but (and that's a massive *but*) when we talk about the book *Upset the World*, you don't have the right context. Without that, you won't totally grasp the implications of what I believe God is trying to do with the Basement.

This is an opportunity to give you a broader context of the vehicle by which we can upset people around us so we can all, together, upset the world.

So, would you be opposed to me having something of a do-over? Because that's what this book is: a reimagined, recontextualized, new take on *Upset the World*.

OPEN VISION

Let me orient you with a vision.

When I was thirty, I had an open vision. Now, before I can move forward, we have to talk about the difference between a vision and a dream.

Obviously, for a dream—a literal dream, not like MLK's "I have a dream"—you're asleep. In your jammies, stretched out on the couch in front of the TV, curled up for a catnap in your car—wherever you are, you are dead to the world, knocked out, *dreaming*.

For a vision, you're awake. In the middle of your day, while you're waiting in line at your preferred coffee shop, staring at the back of the car in front of you at school pickup—in the middle of doing whatever it is that you do, God presses pause on your current physical awareness and gives you a current *spiritual* awareness that takes your understanding of Him and of what He's doing to a whole new level.

The book of Joel is filled with prophecies we can plainly see fulfilled in the New Testament—specifically at Pentecost—but I'm most interested in Joel 2:28:

God presses pause on your current physical awareness and gives you a current spiritual awareness that takes your understanding of Him and of what He's doing to a whole new level.

Then, after doing all those things, I will pour out my Spirit upon
all people. Your sons and daughters will prophesy. Your old men
will dream dreams, and your young men will see visions.

Even in that verse, as Joel is discussing dreams *and* visions, one
is not better than the other. In one you *just happen* to be asleep as
the message is being communicated, and in the other you *just happen* to be wide awake.

I can't argue with what's right there on the page in Scripture.
God can send me a vision.

All right, that said, when I was thirty, God gave me an open
vision. I already have a litty (slang for "enlightened" or "active")
imagination, but this is the only time this has ever happened in my
life, so it stands out with ridiculous clarity in my mind.

I'm walking down a street and I see a hundred-story building in front
of me. All white, scraping the sky. And even though I'm standing
on the ground just looking up at the building, I can clearly hear the
babble of voices, laughter, and music coming from the penthouse, like
I have a direct audio link to the hundredth floor. (Don't ask me how I
can hear it—I know it defies the laws of science—but in visions things
just *happen*.)

When I walk into the building, everything is a sterile white. No art.
No signage. Nothing.

But I can see where the elevator is.

So I press the button. When I get on, I see a button for *L*—obviously
for the Lobby, the floor I'm on. Right above it is a button that reads
100. There are no floors one through ninety-nine. Just that one other
button. So I hit it.

The elevator starts moving up one hundred floors, and as I'm going higher my ears are popping. More interesting to me is what is happening in my head. The higher I go, the more self-conscious I become. The elevator is going up and up and I'm checking my pants for lint and my shirt for stains. Are my clothes wrinkled? Do I look presentable? I have no idea why, but I am bugging out.

It's only as the elevator reaches the top that I intrinsically know the people in the room at the penthouse level are very significant, influential names in the body of Christ. Each is nameless and faceless in my vision, but on the level of a name that anyone from any flavor of Christian background would know at a glance—someone who has had an indelible impact on the church as a whole.

There is a long hallway from the elevator to a set of three steps that lead down into a lavish penthouse.

I'm talking New York City lavish. Imagine the most posh, swank living room you've ever seen. This place is laid *out*! I can see from inside the elevator that there are people talking and hanging through-out this beautiful living room area, then more outside on the balcony just beyond that, mingling under lights, music going. In reality, I know I wouldn't be able to see everything with such clarity from the oppo-site end of the hallway, but this is God's vision for me and I'm not about to argue with His ability to affect what I see.

I step off the elevator into this long hallway, and in my peripheral vision I can see a line of people on either side of the hall. On my left are the most beautiful women in bikinis that you've ever seen in your entire life.

Wait . . . this is a vision from Jesus? A Christian vision?

Yes. Stay with me.

Each woman is holding a silver charger or a platter. And on these platters are every sin, vice, and weight that you could possibly pick up in life.

I think, *Okay, this is crazy.*

Here's the thing: it's not just one or two or three women—these ladies line the *whole* long hallway, all the way to the penthouse.

To my right are the most fit men you've ever seen. Two percent body fat with massive pecs, abs, muscles, and all wearing Speedos. They also are all holding silver chargers with every sin, vice, and weight. Again, not just two or three—they line the whole hallway on my right.

I'm thinking, *All right. This must be the test. You don't get to be in the penthouse with those very influential people in the body of Christ unless you pass this test of temptation.*

Now for me, if there was going to be an issue, it was not the men on my right side and what they had on their chargers. It most definitely would have been on my left. I know I have to pass this test, so I look down at my feet and I don't look up. I walk in a straight line directly to the stairs leading into the suite.

I make it to the three steps down and look into the penthouse. Each of these influential people in the body of Christ is still talking and mingling.

Now, when you're at a party, even if you're having a good time with friends and family, you'll at least look up when someone new shows up. Whether you know the person or not, your attention has been snagged at least for a brief moment.

But in my vision, I walk in and I'm just standing there, scanning the room. No one even looks up at me.

About eight feet away are these two guys talking. As I look closer at their hands, I notice they're both holding something from one of the chargers. As soon as I recognize what they're holding, one of the dudes talking snaps his attention to me.

He gives me a once-over, head to toe. When he notices I'm not holding something from the chargers, he goes right back to his conversation, having never said a word to me.

That's the only moment anyone made eye contact with me or even acknowledged me. I wait a few more minutes, but then think to myself, *I guess I'm not supposed to be up here!*

I turn around, go back up the three steps, and immediately put my head down because now the line of bikini-clad girls is on my right and the line of men in Speedos is on my left. I walk all the way back down the hallway without looking up and make it back to the elevator. I get ready to press the *L* button to go back down to the lobby. But right when I start to press the *L*, I notice a new button under it that simply says *B*.

It's not even a bright, bold *B*. It's faint. Barely there. Not even lit up. As a matter of fact, I never even noticed it on my way up to the penthouse.

So I press the *B*.

Instead of going down one hundred floors, I actually end up going down one hundred *and one* floors.

My ears are going off the whole way down—*Pop! Pop! Pop!*

I get all the way down to what I now know is the basement. If you've ever been in an elevator when it hits the last floor, the basement, you know the weight of the lift just rests different when it reaches its destination. I feel that weight rest and before the doors even open, I can hear laughter, music, lively conversation. It's a party!

One of the very interesting things about the gathering in the penthouse was that up there, it was just the personalities themselves. The people on their own. No wives, no husbands, no children, no friends brought along for fun.

When the doors open to the basement, it's husbands, wives, men, women, kids, friends, siblings, cousins, aunties, uncles—just *everyone.* And as soon as the doors open, everyone's attention immediately swings to the elevators and they start cheering at the top of their lungs. They go *crazy*. A few of them reach into the elevator and pull me out, and they start hugging me and shaking me and patting me on the back.

And they're all saying things like, "Oh my goodness, we're so grateful you made it!"

Through the congratulatory atmosphere, one guy grabs me by both shoulders and kind of shakes me a little. He says, "Bro, welcome. Not everybody that goes up there ever makes it down here."

Scene.

That's the whole vision!

I sat there wondering, *Holy Spirit, what was* that?!

The Holy Spirit said, "Tim, everybody—believers!—thinks that the goal is to get to the top. But I haven't called people to get to the top. I've called them to get to the bottom."

My mind was blown with the parallel.

Then He asked me a question. "Tim, if Jesus is the chief cornerstone, what floor would you want to live on?"

I mean, I don't know about you, but if Jesus is the cornerstone, I want to be as close to the foundation of that building as I can possibly get. Even *inside* of it.

He tells me, "Get as many people to the basement as you can."

THE BASEMENT

Did I mention I was only thirty years old at the time? From that moment forward I shared this vision with anyone I mentored or personally discipled. I did the best I could with that mandate, but I didn't have the whole vision—I couldn't see the full scope of what God wanted to do yet. I had zero clue of how many people He wanted in the Basement. I had no idea He wanted that many people even exposed to the philosophy.

Not until the podcast.

So it goes from a couple dozen people I mentored to hundreds of thousands to millions. And out of that huge pool, thousands have embraced the philosophy and consider themselves Dwellers, that is, people who have pressed B. People who would rather go down than up.

Think about a basement in the natural sense. A lot of people redo their basements into an extra living space. I even know a married couple who converted their basement so well no one ever wants to leave that space—it's just so cool and comfortable!

But the traditional purpose of a basement is for safety. People run to a basement during a storm—especially a tornado—because the safest place in the building is within the foundation of the house. Everything from the first floor up is going to get ripped up! The basement ain't going nowhere.

So, what we've done is taken the intangible philosophy of the Holy Spirit's blueprint—not mine—and the physical understanding of a basement—that safe place in a storm—and given it a tangible expression that people can interact with on a daily basis.

Now there is a whole community of people who have pressed B, who are challenging and turning the socially acceptable definition of what it means to be great and climb the ladder upside down. They've said, "I want to live my life the Basement way. I don't want to spend my time being self-conscious, trying to get to the top floor, and then compromising my fidelity to God by picking up sin, by picking up vices, by picking up weights that would hold me down. I want to get as close to Jesus as I can. And if that's below ground level, He's my chief cornerstone. I want to be next to Him."

What we do from day to day and from week to week—not only through the podcast but each of us through our personal interactions—creates a safe space where people feel comfortable giving us the gift of their vulnerability. Vulnerability is an extravagant gift that you could never demand; you can only create a safe environment to receive it. And if someone feels safe enough to choose to give you that gift, that's something you cherish, steward, and honor.

In life, we're taught that the only way to be great is to go up. I want to challenge that. In the coming chapters, you will learn that the way up is *down*. We're going to talk about the fact that the vision of the Basement is an allegory for how the kingdom itself is upside down—literally "upset," but we'll get to that.

Since receiving this vision, I've spent my life turning other people's lives upside down by upsetting something in their well-ordered understanding of God and the world around them. Everything I have learned about living an upside-down life is in these pages.

I'm finally ready to share it with you. All of it.

Thank you for feeling safe enough to come here. This is a vulnerable moment, and every page turn will be another vulnerable moment. But I'm here with you, and I'm ready to be vulnerable with you. Welcome to the Basement.

Vulnerability is an extravagant gift that you could never demand; you can only create a safe environment to receive it.

one

STUNNING UPSETS

*D*o you believe in miracles?! Yes!"

Overcome with the excitement of the moment, that was all Al Michaels could get out in the final countdown of the USA versus Soviet Union hockey playoff at the 1980 Winter Olympic Games. The whole world had its eyes on Lake Placid, New York, as they watched an underdog team clinch one of the biggest upsets in sports history.

Looking at the two teams going into the game, the Soviets were the *obvious* pick, right? We're talking about seasoned players in their prime—some of whom could easily be listed as among the greatest hockey players *in the world*.

Meanwhile, the Soviet bench was up against a ragtag team made up mostly of college students. I mean, the average age of the American team was twenty-two.

You read that right—*twenty-two*. They were *babies*!

Anyone picking Team USA for the win that day—for anything

other than nostalgia or national pride—would have been straight-up *crazy*. Why?

Expectation.

But that day every single person's expectation got turned upside down—*absolutely* upset.

Why do we call these kinds of wins "upsets"? Because we don't expect them to happen.

When most people think of the word "upset," they think of an emotion.

Someone cut me off in traffic—I'm *upset*.

A toddler is throwing a tantrum in the middle of the grocery store—they are *upset*.

My wife is in her feelings about something—she is *upset*.

Whether there is an offense with your in-laws, your kids are driving you nuts, or your neighbors are getting too rowdy, "upset" has become the common theme of the world lately. Look outside the four walls of your house for just a moment—wars, the government making decisions you don't agree with (no matter which side of the aisle you sit on), racial and social tension in our streets . . .

Everyone is upset about something.

As I started writing this, it was summer of 2022. In just the past two years—for real—we'd seen only *two* Christmases . . . *two* Fourth of Julys . . . *two* Thanksgivings.

Just two.

But just from the beginning of 2020 until now we've experienced a lot of upsetting things.

A worldwide pandemic that shut down life as we knew it. Economic collapse—a couple of times over. The resurgence of a race war that the majority of White America thought was dead and

2

forgotten (it wasn't, and it's nothing new, but that's a conversation for another book). An attack on our capitol by her own citizens. A war in Eastern Europe that threatened to engulf the international political climate in a third world war. There is a *lot* to be upset about . . . *if* what you mean by "upset" is angry, bothered, agitated, or distressed.

But is that what "upset" really means?

Now, don't get me wrong. We all have a right to our emotions and a legal right to protest—I'm not challenging that—but if you're just angry, what is that going to accomplish? I want you to think about this.

At the end of the day, if all you're going to do is talk about how angry you are, what actual impact does that have on the world around you?

What are you changing?

I can almost guarantee you that your anger—on its own—won't do anything except maybe make your face red (depending on your melanin).

Since this whole book hinges on you having the correct working definition and concept of the word "upset," I want to make sure that as we get started, you know exactly what I'm talking about—*without a shadow of a doubt*. I've looked at multiple dictionaries just to make sure I'm right. Across every dictionary I could find, the definition could be synthesized to this:

> Upset (v.): 1. to overturn, to destroy the power of, to overthrow, to defeat, or to vanquish. 2. to disturb or derange completely; to put out of order, to throw into disorder.

The majority of people tend to focus on the second definition.

Deranged completely? Thrown into disorder? Who would want this to happen in their life?

This is why I want to address the definition, as we handle it, because whatever previous experience you have with "upset," *that* is the understanding you will carry into the coming chapters.

That understanding is what I'm here to challenge.

The first or primary definition of "upset" literally means to "overturn" or, in other words, to turn upside down.

Take a cup. Pour a little water into it. Set it down. Now turn it over (over a sink, preferably—I'm not trying to make your momma or your spouse mad). That's it! You've upset the cup. It's just that simple . . . *and* just that complicated.

Because that's what happens when Jesus comes into your life. Everything gets turned upside down—or, rather, from heaven's perspective, *right side up.*

This is the core of the vision God showed me about the Basement. Everyone is trying so hard to be great and get to the top, the penthouse. What they don't recognize is that their understanding of what it means to be great needs to be upset.

THE CHALLENGE

What I'd really like to do with you in this book is challenge your understanding of this single word and take a deeper look at what it means to be upset and to upset those around you—not for the purpose of stirring up more anger and strife, but to change and impact the world around you . . . for the better. To bring as many people to the Basement as you can.

Throughout this book we're going to talk about a few topics, just

As you read,
you might get
uncomfortable—
that's okay. That's
the feeling of
something in your
life facing an upset.

like we do on the podcast. I'm going to tell you a couple stories and we'll maybe even have a little fun along the way. My chapters aren't long because I believe in the sanctity of brevity.

I also might ask you a few questions—as a matter of fact, I *will* ask you a few questions. Get out your notebook. Prepare to take notes. There will be a quiz for the nerds.

There's also space after each chapter where I'll ask you a few questions to probe deeper into what's upsetting you and provide space where you can take notes about what's going on in your heart and mind. Even about what Jesus is saying to you about what you just read.

As you read, you might get uncomfortable—that's okay. That's the feeling of *something* in your life facing an upset.

What you do next with that feeling is entirely up to you.

Are you ready? *Let's go* . . .

Practical Matters

So you won't be nervous, this is what a questions page will look like. Here's your first one:

Have you witnessed any stunning upsets in your life?

_____

_____

_____

_____

_____

_____

Is there something in your life God wants to upset?

_____

_____

_____

_____

_____

_____

_____

_____

Notes

What is God saying to you?

_____

_____

_____

_____

_____

_____

_____

_____

_____

part one

WHY BE UPSET?

Two

UPSIDE DOWN

So we're talking about living a life that's been overturned, turned upside down by the power, the presence, and the love of Jesus Christ. And, because of that, how you can use that life to turn the world upside down and bring more people to the Basement.

But before we rush into anything, I want to take the time to break this down a little. Let's start with Paul and Silas.

Paul and Silas then traveled through the towns of Amphipolis and Apollonia and came to Thessalonica, where there was a Jewish synagogue. As was Paul's custom, he went to the synagogue service, and for three Sabbaths in a row he used the Scriptures to reason with the people. He explained the prophecies and proved that the Messiah must suffer and rise from the dead. He said, "This Jesus I'm telling you about is the Messiah." Some of the Jews who listened were persuaded and joined Paul and Silas, along with many God-fearing Greek men and quite a few prominent women.

But some of the Jews were jealous, so they gathered some troublemakers from the marketplace to form a mob and start a riot. They attacked the home of Jason, searching for Paul and Silas so they could drag them out to the crowd. Not finding them there, they dragged out Jason and some of the other believers instead and took them before the city council. "Paul and Silas have *caused trouble all over the world*," they shouted, "and now *they are here disturbing our city, too*. And Jason has welcomed them into his home. They are all guilty of treason against Caesar, for they profess allegiance to another king, named Jesus."

The people of the city, as well as the city council, were thrown into turmoil by these reports. So the officials forced Jason and the other believers to post bond, and then they released them.

—ACTS 17:1–9

If you pick up the New King James Version or the English Standard Version (or if you grew up reading the King James Version like I did, which just sticks in my memory), it says Paul and Silas have turned the world "upside down." But the word in Greek—the language the book of Acts was originally written in—literally means "to upset." Instead of "caused trouble" in verse 6, that phrase could be translated, "they caused the world to be *upset*, and now they are here disturbing our city, too."

But . . . why be upset? Why would you want to live your life turned upside down? Who wants to do that—live in an entirely different way than you're living right now? Who *wants* to go to the Basement initially? Aren't we all trying to make it to the top?

I'm a bit of a literalist, so I love definitions—*a lot*. Just in case you're not a nerd like me and you weren't paying attention the first time, I want to give you the definition of "upset" again so you have

Who wants
to go to the
Basement
initially?
Aren't we all
trying to make
it to the top?

the necessary context for the coming pages. (Even if you did read it the first time—#nerdsruletheworld #youshouldbetakingnotes—read it again, just so it sticks.)

> Upset (v.): 1. to overturn, to destroy the power of, to overthrow, to defeat, or to vanquish. 2. to disturb, or derange completely; to put out of order, to throw into disorder.

The definition in dictionaries always goes on to give a few examples, like upsetting a system, a mechanism, or an apartment, or defeating a more formidable opponent in war, politics, or sports, as we talked about already (see, nerds *do* rule the world).

WHY BE UPSET?

Well, truth is that there are people all over the world who somehow made a commitment to have their lives turned upside down—even me. I came to a revelation that I was not living my life the way I should be. I was determined to make it to the penthouse, but through Scripture and through an understanding of what it means to have a relationship with Jesus Christ, I found out what so many others—to the tune of more than *two and a half billion people* (by most recent records)—have discovered: that my life should not be lived the way I want it but the way that He wants me to live it. This threw the way I'd lived my whole life up until that point into chaos and disorder until I landed in the Basement.

Look back at the italicized statement in that quote from Acts 17 for just a second. I wonder if the Jews in that city had any idea how wildly exaggerative and unintentionally prophetic their words were.

Paul and Silas hadn't turned the whole world upside down—they're in freaking Thessalonica. It's not like the Jews in this city were getting letters from the tip of Latin America . . . it's been only thirty years since Jesus' death. You're telling me Paul and Silas did a lap around *the whole world*—mostly walking—and made it back to *this tiny city*? Suuuuure . . .

Come on. Stop.

That being said, it is a wildly exaggerative and unintentionally prophetic comment for that moment. That now, over two thousand years later, what they said out of their melodrama is *still* happening—all over the world. The gospel is still invading people's cities and turning lives upside down with the message, love, and hope of Jesus Christ.

It's happening in every city. In every country. In every tribe. In every language. Every day.

That a couple of angry Jewish guys could make a wild statement that was both untrue and true at the same time . . . *Man*, I just think God has a sense of humor!

Listen, I know there are a lot of people who might put this book down right now. If living their life for Jesus means they have to make hard lifestyle choices and changes in their habits, the places they go, and the people they spend time with—not only is that something they're not really into, that's the *last* thing they want. They are on their way to the penthouse and their minds will not be changed; they will not be stopped!

But can I challenge you to stick around for a moment? I want to give you what I believe are my top three reasons why you should be upset and why you should give permission to God to come in and turn your life—your *everything*—upside down.

The gospel is still invading people's cities and turning lives upside down with the message, love, and hope of Jesus Christ.

Scripture Reference

Acts 17:1–9

Practical Matters

Is there any area in your life that God might be poking at? An area where you think He might be inspiring you to change?

_____

_____

_____

_____

_____

_____

Why would you want to live your life turned upside down?

_____

_____

_____

_____

Notes

What is God saying to you?

_____

_____

_____

_____

_____

_____

_____

_____

_____

_____

_____

_____

_____

_____

_____

_____

_____

Three

SPOILER ALERT

I think the majority of people reading this probably know John 3:16, but I'm still going to put it in here in ink and on paper for God's and for posterity's sake because good nerds take notes. I'll say it again: nerds rule the world!

> For this is how God loved the world: He gave his one and only Son, so that everyone who believes in him will not perish but have eternal life.

My main reason why you should have your life upset, why you should give your life to God?

Because He is *madly* in love with you.

Now, that might seem basic. You're probably thinking, *No duh, Tim. I know.* But this is something that has to be at the absolute forefront of your mind as we start this journey because if you don't know that God loves you, then you will live your life—or attempt to live your life—for *all the wrong reasons.*

If you don't live your life from a standpoint of understanding God's love for you, then you'll live it from a standpoint of fear. Everything you do and say will be informed by the ethos of "I have to do everything God says or else He'll strike me down."

But God is a God of love, and He loves us in a way that is so profound that it should cause us to be upset.

YOU

Look at Ephesians 1:4–5:

> Even before he made the world, God loved us . . .

Hold up. Stop right there for *just* a second. I know, I know . . . I interrupted a scripture, but there's something I want to make sure you're catching. That statement right there should make at least twenty-five people reading this book have a *party.* Even before He made the world—think about that . . .

Even before He said, "Let there be light," He loved you.

Before He called out a creature, He *loved* you.

Before He pointed to the ground and said, "cockroach," or to the sky and said, "pterodactyl," He had *you* on His mind.

Before you did anything that would disqualify you from a relationship with Him, He was already in love with *you.* That's good news!

Okay. Back to our scripture:

> . . . and chose us in Christ to be holy and without fault in his eyes. God decided in advance to adopt us into his own family

Before you did anything that would disqualify you from a relationship with Him, He was already in love with you. That's good news!

by bringing us to himself through Jesus Christ. This is what he wanted to do, and it gave him great pleasure.

—EPHESIANS 1:4–5

This—coming to humanity in the flesh of a human, not just manifesting as a grown man but coming as an *infant* in a manger and living out every hard moment of childhood and adolescence and puberty and young adulthood and adult life—is what He *wanted* to do.

This—coming so that he could experience every hard moment we would ever experience: every conflict, every sickness, every temptation, every hunger, every need that we would ever see or know—was *not* against His will.

Now let's go to Romans 8. But first, I'd like to clear something up.

THIS IS NOT PREDESTINATION

When you read a phrase like "God decided to do something in advance," a lot of people get stuck on predestination. It's been a conversation in the church for centuries, but if you're not familiar with it, according to the Oxford dictionary, "predestination" is "the divine foreordaining of all that will happen, especially with regard to the salvation of some and not others."[1] In other words, predestination states the idea that God foreknew and predestined whether or not each of us would be saved.

Predestination seems to say, "God decided to do this, and I really don't have a choice in the matter. The people that are going to be saved *are* going to be saved, and there's nothing that we can do about it. The people that aren't going to be saved *aren't* going to be saved, and there's also nothing we can do about it—and God *fixed* it like this." In other words, predestination implies that the people in church, in the Basement right now, are the people He *wanted*. And the people that are not in a relationship with Him, He decided a long time ago that He didn't want anything to do with them. Before you had a choice to say anything about it, God just arbitrarily decided, "I don't want you in . . . I don't like the way you dress. I don't like the way you talk. I don't like *you*."

Petty.

But we just talked about how much He loves us, so this couldn't be further from the truth!

What happens in this instance is that people get fixed on predestination and completely forget about God's *foreknowledge*.

FOREKNOWLEDGE = SPOILER

I want to show you the clearest, most concise scriptures to give you context for what this means—which brings us to Romans 8:

> And we know that God causes everything to work together for the good of those who love God and are called according to his purpose for them. For God knew his people in advance, and he chose them to become like his Son, so that his Son would be the firstborn among many brothers and sisters. And having chosen them, he called them to come to him. And having called them, he gave them right standing with himself. And having given them right standing, he gave them his glory.
>
> —VERSES 28–30

The King James Version says, "Whom he called, them he also justified: and whom he justified, them he also glorified" (verse 30). Feel free to read that with the echoing cadence of an old-school Baptist preacher. I love the King James Version—it just makes everything sound a little bit more elegant, eloquent, and intelligent.

Here's the good news: God isn't trying to rig something in a way that kicks some people out and keeps some people in.

Let's not forget the sovereignty of God—He's the Alpha and the Omega. He's the beginning and the end, the first and the last.

But maybe you'll understand foreknowledge in a different way. In today's culture it's called a "spoiler alert."

THAT MOVIEGOER

Have you ever gone to a movie with a person who's already seen the film you're seeing? And for some reason, the person *can't help* but tell you not only that they already saw the movie but also something that gives away a pivotal plot point or—God forbid—the entire ending? After that, all you can say is, "I hate you. Why did I even come with you?" That conversation would have called for a spoiler alert.

The person already saw the movie, so they already know the ending. Once they tell you the ending, there's nothing you can do to make a difference in the movie. "Yoda can't die. In Jesus' name, Yoda won't die! He will live and declare the goodness—"

Stop. No one's that spiritual watching *Return of the Jedi*, okay?

Spoiler alert! That person didn't *fix* the ending, and neither can you. They just knew it. And now you do too.

That's foreknowledge.

Predestination is someone saying, "I'm going to make *sure* this happens, and there's nothing you can do about it." Foreknowledge is that person saying, "I know everything that's going to happen anyway."

God already knows whose heart is going to be soft enough to even come into a relationship with Him.

He already knows those people, and since He does, He's predestined it so they have an encounter with Jesus Christ. It's like He's saying, "Because I foreknew it, I'm calling them. Because I'm calling them, I'm sanctifying them. And because I'm sanctifying them, they're going to end up right back here with Me in the Basement."

That's not God *rigging* souls, letting a few people in and keeping a bunch of people out just because He's God.

HE KNOWS HIS KIDS

You know how I know? Because I couldn't do that with *my* kids. I have some limited foreknowledge of my kids based on their personalities. I've spent enough time with them to know their behavioral traits. In other words, I know which child is predisposed to do what thing.

If someone came into my office and told me, "I'm sorry, Mr. Ross, one of your kids just did (fill in the blank)." I could come within 95 percent accuracy of telling you which kid did it.

If you came to me and said, "Hey, one of your kids is outside bossing everyone around, acting like he's the parent," I'd go, "That's Nathan."

But if someone came to me and said one of my children was jumping off the roof of my car, I'd just know that's Noah. (Because Nathan would take one look at the car and the jump and go, "That's

God's big enough to know everything and set the world based on what He already knew.

high. That hurts. No thank you." He takes after his daddy!) Noah, on the other hand, is the bravest person on the planet. We tell him, "Look both ways before you cross the street!" And the boy just *walks* into the street, confident as you please. "There are no cars, Daddy!"

My sons have been with me for only thirteen years and fifteen years. Because they're my children, I know their mannerisms, their attributes, their tendencies, and their leanings. I know my kids. I know one would never do this and I know the other would, but look, I'm just a *natural* daddy and my knowledge is based on the limited time I have with my children.

We're talking about a heavenly Father. Creator of all beings across all time. Of course He knows *before*! God's big enough to know everything and set the world based on what He already knew. If we go down the discussion rabbit hole that He doesn't just fore-know and everything that happens is some divine machination, then His actions are not out of love—they're out of something else. That is the kind of puppetry that I don't want to be a part of.

God's not up there rigging our minds to behave in a certain way just so He can make a comparative analysis about two of His kids. He's not rubbing His chin, mumbling, "Hmmm, I'll make this one bad and send him down a bad path so I can purposefully set him up against this one who's on a good path, *just* to highlight how different they are." That's not how He works.

If it's all predetermined, then free will doesn't actually exist, and that's not a game *anyone* really wants to play. Period.

Think of it like this: God is the director of the movie. He chose the cast, and He has the whole script, but they get to decide what lines they read. He knows how the movie starts and how it ends. But if you know anything about the movie industry and how a film is produced, then you know that even though production starts with a full script in everyone's hands, lines get rewritten all the time throughout preproduction and filming based on how the story is developing and how the actors portray the characters.

Here's just one example: Aaron Paul plays Jesse Pinkman opposite Bryan Cranston's Walter White in the show *Breaking Bad* (if you're appalled that I'm talking about a secular show, even *this* secular show, you're really not going to like me after chapters 7 through 9, but moving on . . .). The original script had Jesse Pinkman in only the first two episodes. He winds up in all five seasons! Aaron Paul ended up being the second-strongest star in the series behind Cranston. There was something his performance brought to the narrative that changed the director's decision on how this character's story was going to play out.

Though the director starts filming with a knowledge of the script, as that's playing out in real time he's surprised as he sees Aaron Paul really taking on the role. "Wow!" I imagine the director saying. "I didn't think you were going to play this role that well! I didn't know you were going to light up the screen like that!"

Not only is he surprised but so is the actor! "I didn't know this was going to happen—I only signed up for two episodes! I need to go change my whole schedule now!"

With God as the author and finisher of our faith, He knows the end from the beginning, just like the director of a television series. What we can't get our finite human minds around is the ability for our free will to have been floating around in His head, coexisting with His foreknowledge. Our minds are just too finite to even grasp or deal with it. In our tiny minds, God's foreknowledge and our free will are so contradictory they can't even exist in the same room let alone in the same divine mind. You could sit for a hundred moons and you would be no closer to understanding it than the first day you started pondering. It's a sovereign thing and there's just no way for us to know it.

But in spite of everything, He loves us? That's mind-blowing!

So why be upset? Because He's in love with you, and He went to great lengths to prove it.

Oops—spoiler alert . . .

Scripture References

John 3:16
Ephesians 1:4–5
Romans 8:28–30

Practical Matters

Maybe it was hard hearing that God knows all the spoilers for your life. I don't know about you, but it would have been nice to know ahead of time about some of the hard things I've been through.

What are some moments in your life when you could have used a spoiler, when you maybe felt God wasn't around or looking out for you?

_____

_____

_____

_____

_____

How can you reframe those moments, knowing now that God was there with you the whole time?

_____

_____

_____

_____

_____

_____

_____

Notes

What is God saying to you?

_____

_____

_____

_____

_____

_____

_____

four

OFF OF A MAYBE

Okay, so we're still in Romans, but if you would, flip your Bible back just a bit to chapter 5:

> When we were utterly helpless, Christ came at just the right time and died for us sinners. Now, most people would not be willing to die for an upright person, though someone *might perhaps* be willing to die for a person who is especially good. But God showed his great love for us by sending Christ to die for us while we were still sinners.
>
> —VERSES 6–8

While we were still sinners, before we ever had our minds on Him, God sent His Son to die for us.

Get this—off of a *maybe*.

This is the most upsetting thing to me. It's the thing that turned my life upside down.

Off of a maybe.

While we were still sinners, before we ever had our minds on Him, God sent His Son to die for us. Get this—off of a maybe.

IT'S NOT A HAUNTING

Imagine God looking at the world and saying to us, way far into any possible future, "I'm going to send My Son to die on a cross—a traumatic and barbaric death—because *perhaps* you'll hear. You'll hear about the gospel, and *perhaps* you'll give your life to Jesus Christ. It's worth letting My Son bleed out on a cross off of a maybe."

Who does that?!

I'm going to be very real with you and say I wouldn't come to *lunch* if you told me *maybe* you'd show up. Wouldn't even set a date for it.

If you came to me and said, "Hey, man, I'd like to spend some time talking with you. Would you want to grab lunch on Tuesday?" I'd pull out my calendar, and we'd decide on Tuesday at the Cheesecake Factory—my favorite place. Cool. I'm getting my tastebuds ready for a good meal and my spirit ready for a good conversation.

But if I asked what time you wanted to meet and you responded with, "I don't know . . . I *might* get there at some point during the day," I'm not coming.

I couldn't do Jesus' job! Because if I did, you would *have* to serve me!

There'd be no chance for you to get over your agnosticism . . . or your atheism . . . or all the questions you have . . . or your hurts and wounds from previous church experiences.

I would *haunt* you. You would wake up every morning, and I'd be right there—in your face.

"Do you love me today? How about today?" Pointing to my hands, "See this hole? See this one? I did this for you." I would just *stalk* you! Every day until you finally went, "OKAY, JESUS!"

Listen, this is just how my brain works. I see everything in pictures—everything I read, everything I hear. These images aren't just for the sake of this book—this is actually how I *think*, how I process my own understanding of the Bible. I also happen to be the type of person who will go to great lengths to help other people see the pictures that are in my head. Sometimes to their chagrin. (You're welcome.)

So when I read the Bible, I imagine myself in Jesus' role in His narrative. As an empath, I often find myself standing in His shoes, wondering how I'd feel or respond in that same situation.

When it comes to me thinking about being Savior or Lord, I would just never give you a choice. Ever.

If I died for *you*, your love in return would have to be nonnegotiable. You've got no choice. That's it!

But somehow, that's just not how He works.

Can you imagine how loving He actually is? That He went up on that cross and bled out off of a *maybe*?

That should upset someone besides me, right?

RED RAIN

Okay, don't judge me for this. Consider that my disclaimer. When the scripture says, "Most people would not be willing to die for an upright person, though someone might perhaps be willing to die for a person who is especially good" (verse 7), I immediately think of the lyrics from a song called "I Would Die 4 U," by Prince and the Revolution.[1] I'd quote the entire thing here if I could, but I really don't need any copyright issues on my back. So if you're not already familiar with it and you're not opposed to a little Google search or Spotify query, check out the song on your

Can you imagine how loving He actually is? That He went up on that cross and bled out off of a maybe?

preferred streaming service or look up the lyrics. It's a *sermon*. In it, Prince sings to a woman about a love so deep that he would die for her—he even talks about that sacrificial love in terms of being a messiah (I can't even *joke* about that!) and needing this girl he loves to *believe* his love.

Y'all, I'm dancing in my seat just *thinking* about this song (how could I not?) because it honestly seems like Prince was on to something. Seriously, if you haven't yet, pause here and go check out that song if you don't already know it. He is *preaching* in these lyrics.

Currently, my message point and I are either more endeared to you because of my Prince reference, or you hate me, you think I'm irreverent because I related Prince's lyrics to the Bible, and I've lost you completely.

Don't worry—we're not singing Prince's songs in a worship service. I point you to these lyrics because I want you to think about something that you might not see at first glance. I'm a lyricist, so when I listen to music, I hear the words first and the melody second. As I'm listening, these lyrics have me thinking: *This dude wrote some verses about dying for this girl to get her to* maybe *understand how into her he was. To* maybe *respond in kind.*

Let me tell you the good news about the gospel: Jesus didn't wait to see if you *wanted* Him to. The good news of the gospel is that before you even knew to ask the question, Christ decided to die for your sins.

It's the most upsetting thing that's ever happened in all of human history. Not because it makes anyone angry, but because it presents this amazing opportunity for a shift in a person's life, an invitation to the Basement, all off of a *maybe*.

And that "maybe" is you.

Scripture Reference

Romans 5:6–8

Practical Matters

Have you ever heard a song on the radio or read a book and thought, *That'll preach*, because it so closely resembles the sacrificial nature of what Jesus did on the cross?

_____

_____

_____

_____

_____

_____

Take a moment and ask God to help you see His presence as you go about your day and to show you how He shows up in even the most mundane things of life.

_____

_____

_____

_____

_____

Notes

What is God saying to you?

_____

_____

_____

_____

_____

_____

_____

_____

_____

_____

_____

_____

_____

_____

_____

_____

_____

_____

five

THE REASON WHY
WE'RE ALL HERE

I'd like to share two scriptures I believe prove that God has plans for you—one from the Old Testament and one from the New.

You might know these scriptures already, but I'd still like to include them here because when you know the address of a scripture, it's not just you claiming, "Somewhere in the Bible, it says God has plans for me." When you know *exactly* where it is, it gives you something to stand on when the enemy—Satan—comes against you and tries to overthrow you.

Here's the Old Testament promise:

"For I know the plans I have for you," says the LORD. "They are plans for good and not for disaster, to give you a future and a hope."

—JEREMIAH 29:11

If you look at that verse, it tells you a couple of things: (1) God loves you. Why? (2) Because He has plans for you. There's something He wants you to *do* with your life.

Here is the promise again, restated in the New Testament:

> For we are God's masterpiece. He has created us anew in Christ Jesus, so we can do the good things he planned for us long ago.
>
> —EPHESIANS 2:10

This is one of my favorites. *We are God's masterpiece.*

A WORK OF ART

Just as a random question—how many people do you think actually believe that? Don't feel pressure to raise your hand—you're probably reading alone, and I know you likely don't want to anyway. Being a masterpiece is hard to wrap your mind around because, you know what? You kind of live with yourself.

Do you know the saying, "Everywhere you go, *there* you are"? Sometimes we can be in a season of life where it's hard for us to even begin to embrace the truths God says about us.

But you *are* a masterpiece.

And that's not my opinion. We just saw that scripture says we are created new in Christ Jesus so we could do the things that He planned for us long ago.

Did you know that when you give your life to Jesus, when you allow Him to come into your life and turn everything upside down, when you decide to be upset by God's love in Jesus' death, He throws a massive party?

We are
God's
masterpiece.

The party I saw in the vision of the Basement doesn't even come close to what's happening in heaven when you make that decision, but this is how I imagine it in my mind:

God goes, "*Yes!*" His arms fly in the air, and He starts break dancing. He's walking around slapping fives with all the angels. He's leading the angels in a chant, "It's about to go down! It's about to go down!"

Maybe one angel walks up—because somehow he's out of the loop, and this guy's excitement is too much to ignore—and he asks, "What's about to go down?"

"Oh, you have *no* idea!" says God over all the cheering. "Tim just gave his life to Jesus!"

"*What?*" The clueless angel is eight kinds of confused and it's *loud* in here.

"*Tim* just gave his life to Jesus!"

"Tim? *That* dude down there?" I can just see the perturbed look on the angel's face.

"Yes, that dude down there, the one who got molested when he was eight. That guy just gave his life to Jesus—had his whole life upset!"

"The guy who was a porn addict?" The angel *really* just doesn't get it.

"Yes! It's going *down*! I got plans for him!" God's excitement is visible. He's *bouncing* with it.

The angel maybe cocks an eyebrow in continued confusion. "You've got plans for *him*? The molested porn addict?" He just doesn't comprehend.

"Yes!" God is still fist pumping, and His excitement is starting to catch on, the angel finally beginning to crack a smile as the excitement bubbles over and into him. "Yes, I've got plans for him!

I've got plans for people who were alcoholics and substance abusers and used to get high every day. I've got plans for people who were bitter, angry, held grudges—who were just mad for no reason every day. I've got plans for *everybody*. It's just a matter of if they're going to be upset or not because they don't have to stay the way they were."

If the angel asked what plans God had for me, I'd imagine Him maybe rubbing His chin a little with a smile and pulling out my report card from kindergarten.

"Timmy is nice," my kindergarten teacher wrote, "but he won't stay in his seat. In the middle of his classwork, he gets up and tries to help the whole class with their work—but he's not even really done with his own work!"

She wasn't wrong. At five years old, I'd self-appointed myself to be the teacher's aide.

I'd write my name at the top of my page, then, "Hey, Bobby! You good? Good! A B C . . . You're doing good, buddy! Sharon, you all right? And two plus two is four . . . All right . . ."

Meanwhile, the teacher is asking me to cut that out, and I just don't see what the big deal is. I'm just trying to help!

I'm betting God took one look at that and saw *me*: Talks a lot, really loud, won't calm down. Can't talk without all this animation. What to do with a guy like that?

Let's make him a preacher.

"Hilarious," says the angel. "You know he wants to be in law enforcement like his mom, right?"

And maybe God just nods. "Yeah, I know he wants to be in law enforcement—that's the plan *he* made for himself. My plans are way better than his plans."

Now, if I really wanted to push my own way onto the police force in Los Angeles, God would have let me because He doesn't interfere in that way. (Remember, I can change the script—that's free will.) But instead, He foreknew who I was and set it up so that I had an encounter with Him, and just waited to see what happened after that.

He has a plan for surfers, librarians, IT nerds, neurosurgeons, and video game guys like me. He has a plan for all of us.

SHOWPIECE

A lot of people think God's not using them unless they're preaching from a pulpit, but listen, His plans are so profound and strategic that they touch people all over the world in all industries. Jesus didn't die so that everyone could be in the pulpit preaching—there are exponentially more people in the marketplace than there will ever be in leadership in the church. So He strategically places us and plans to use each of us within our areas of expertise, that singular place of our passion, to reach people for His name.

I had the gift of upsetting someone in my own life that way. My wife, Juliette.

I laid eyes on her in February of 1998. Said hi to her in April. I told her I liked her in May. Told her I loved her in June. I don't know about you, but that's a pretty fast timeline.

That "I love you" happened on Father's Day. I'll never forget it.

When I told her I loved her, Juliette started laughing in my face. No joke. I'm pouring out my heart to her, and she cracked up.

I had made this card and put all these mushy words in it. I handed it to her before church—that way, she could meditate on the Scriptures *and* read this love letter from me.

After service I walked up to her and said, "Hey, did you read the card?"

"Yeah," she said, "but I want *you* to read it."

Here I am (all bravado) thinking, *Ain't nobody scared of you.* So I start reading the card but then—and take notes, gentlemen—I put the card behind my back and said, "Girl, I don't need to read what's on this card because it's already written on my heart." And I said the rest of the words from memory.

It ended with me saying, "Juliette, I, Timothy Charles Ross, am in love with you."

Her response?

"Bahahaha!"

You've got to have a lot of self-esteem to handle being that vulnerable and then get laughed at.

She told me, "I'm not in love with you. You're a nice guy. If you died, I'd cry. But I'm not in love with you. I've never been in love with anyone. So I'm not in love with you."

Not lying! This really happened.

I looked her in the eyes and said, "I didn't tell you this for you to be in love with me. I told you so that you would know."

And then I walked away.

Ring a bell?

Now for her side of the story . . .

She was driving that night, talking to God, saying, "I'm not in love with that guy. This is ridiculous."

The Holy Spirit told her, "Yes, you are."

"No, I'm not," she said.

They went back and forth a couple times, and it finally ended when she shouted, "Okay, I am!"

Upside down. Love was expressed upside down—in a way that defied her expectations—(the Basement way)—and it literally overturned an emotion she was having.

And it was totally natural.

Imagine the spiritual dynamic, the shift in yourself when you realize someone is so in love with you that before you could even express your love to them—before you even truly *understood* it—they communicated their love to you in such an outrageously extravagant way: letting their Son die on a cross for you.

That kind of shift can inspire you to literally upset the world around you.

Scripture References

Jeremiah 29:11
Ephesians 2:10

Practical Matters

Do you find it hard to believe that you are God's masterpiece? Spend some time talking to God about what He says about you.

_____

_____

_____

_____

_____

_____

_____

Imagine the spiritual dynamic, the shift in yourself when you realize someone is so in love with you that before you could even express your love to them—before you even truly understood it—they communicated their love to you.

Scriptures for Thought

Psalm 18:32

Psalm 139:14

Romans 8:37–39

1 Corinthians 3:16

2 Corinthians 5:12

2 Corinthians 5:20

Ephesians 2:10

1 Thessalonians 1:4

2 Timothy 1:7

1 John 3:1

Notes

What is God saying to you?

_____

_____

_____

_____

_____

_____

_____

_____

_____

_____

_____

_____

_____

part Two

RELIGION
DOESN'T WORK

six

SORRY, NOT SORRY

*A*ll right, so we've already established that this book, at its core, is about the true sense of words. All of my nerds should be nodding. Here's a new word for discussion on this journey: "religion."

I've heard a lot of talk in the past decade or so about "religion versus relationship." People don't want anything to do with religion—they just want a relationship with Jesus, so they say, "Jesus wasn't religious." I understand the heart behind what they're attempting to accomplish, but the fact of the matter is that this statement couldn't be further from the truth.

Jesus was a devout Jewish rabbi. He never missed a festival or a feast—He made them up, after all, and they're all about Him anyway.

We're all "religious." We're religious when we're in church every Sunday. If you have a consistent prayer life or a consistent devotional time with God, then you're religious about carving out time to be in the presence of God. If I go to Saltgrass Steak House, I religiously get the carrot cake. We all have some religious proclivities, so there's nothing wrong with the word itself.

In sermons we tend to treat the ultrareligious Pharisees like they're the bad guys, but they're not actually *bad* guys. They loved God, and they loved His law. They just didn't have an understanding of what it would look like for God to be right in front of them in the form of a man, explaining the laws He gave to those who were trying to follow them in real time.

These weren't bad dudes! They just didn't understand the impact of their experience.

With that said, religion *doesn't work*. The reason why is that religion without the person that you are devoted to or faithful to is empty and worthless.

That's what God hates—empty and faithless religion He's not included in.

HOLLOW

Every Friday night is date night for Juliette and me. Pre-COVID, we went to the movies, dinner, the whole thing—and I *loved* it. During COVID we had to redefine what date night looked like. We'd catch a movie on our favorite streaming service. Now, post-COVID, movies can be at the theater or we can still just watch them on our couch. But we're religious about that night because we're really into each other. Because we're really into each other, we set a date on our calendars to spend time with each other exclusively, and it's beautiful. This is a religious practice I never want to give up.

Now, as beautiful as that religious practice is, imagine if Juliette got up on a Friday and was sick, had a headache, or felt nauseous and begged for that night off. Maybe this is even the *first* night post-COVID that we'd be able to go out. We were going to catch a

Religion without the person that you are devoted to or faithful to is empty and worthless.

movie and sit in the big reclining seats, do dinner out, the whole thing.

Imagine if she says she's sick and can't go, but my response is, "Well, I already bought the tickets. It's Friday. I'm going to the movie with or without you," and then I still go to the movie.

Well, I *could* do that. But now I've put the day itself above my date. I can still go to the movie saying I'm keeping up with the religious practice of going to the movies with Juliette, except . . . she's not with me. And if she's not present, my religion is bad—it's empty.

Just in case someone doesn't understand Him the first time (or, more truthfully, *because* they don't understand), in multiple places in the Old Testament God finds ways to tell His children that he "hates" religious practices (if your religious spirit doubts me, check out Amos 5:21–23 for one).

You might look at any one of those moments and, like the Pharisees, say, "Well, wait a minute, sir! You're the one who told us to do these things. You told us to observe these days!"

Yeah, He did, but because we haven't included Him—He's nowhere to be found—He hates them.

You see, I can look the part of having fun with Juliette, but if I haven't talked to her in a week, what's it worth? I can tell other people I love my wife and sound like I'm in love with her, but if I haven't told *Juliette*, what's the point?

That's why religion on its own doesn't work—it's missing key factors.

JESUS SPIT BARS

There was a day when Jesus got so mad at religion that He absolutely *went off* on some people. And it's probably one of the most gangster scenes in the Bible. As you read the following verses, I want you to pick up on His tone. Perhaps I'm assuming a little bit about what His tone might have been by the exclamation points behind certain words. But I want you to pick up on what He's really getting at here.

To give you some context, Jesus is talking to the crowds and to His disciples, and He's about to put the religious leaders on *blast*. Look at what He says to the crowd.

(Disclaimer: This is probably more verses than you've ever seen together in any other book, but . . . you know. Deal with it.)

Then Jesus said to the crowds and to his disciples, "The teachers of religious law and the Pharisees are the official interpreters of the law of Moses. So practice and obey whatever they tell you, but don't follow their example. For they don't practice what they teach. They crush people with unbearable religious demands and never lift a finger to ease the burden.

"Everything they *do* is for show. . . . They *love* to receive respectful greetings as they walk in the marketplaces, and to be called '*Rabbi*.' . . .

"What sorrow awaits you teachers of religious law and you Pharisees. *Hypocrites*! For you shut the door of the Kingdom of Heaven in people's faces. You won't go in yourselves, and you don't let others enter either.

"What sorrow awaits you teachers of religious law and you Pharisees. *Hypocrites*! For you cross land and sea to make one convert, and then you turn that person into twice the child of hell you yourselves are!

"Blind guides! What sorrow awaits you! For you say that it means nothing to swear 'by God's Temple,' but that it is binding to swear 'by the gold in the Temple.' Blind fools! Which is more important—the gold or the Temple that makes the gold sacred? . . .

"What sorrow awaits you teachers of religious law and you Pharisees. *Hypocrites*! For you are careful to tithe even the tiniest income from your herb gardens, but you ignore the more important aspects of the law—justice, mercy, and faith. You should tithe, yes, but do not neglect the more important things. Blind guides! You strain your water so you won't accidentally swallow a gnat, but you swallow a camel!

"What sorrow awaits you teachers of religious law and you Pharisees. *Hypocrites*! For you are so careful to clean the outside of the cup and the dish, but inside you are filthy—full of greed and self-indulgence! You blind Pharisee! First wash the inside of the cup and the dish, and then the outside will become clean, too.

"What sorrow awaits you teachers of religious law and you Pharisees. *Hypocrites*! For you are like whitewashed tombs—beautiful on the outside but filled on the inside with dead people's bones and all sorts of impurity. Outwardly you look like righteous people, but inwardly your hearts are filled with hypocrisy and lawlessness.

"What sorrow awaits you teachers of religious law and you Pharisees. *Hypocrites*! For you build tombs for the prophets your ancestors killed, and you decorate the monuments of the godly people your ancestors destroyed. Then you say, 'If we had lived in the days of our ancestors, we would never have joined them in killing the prophets.'

"But in saying that, you testify against yourselves that you are indeed the descendants of those who murdered the prophets. Go ahead and finish what your ancestors started. *Snakes*! Sons of *vipers*! How will you escape the judgment of hell?

I have two reasons why religion doesn't work: (1) The look of it and (2) the sound of it.

"Therefore, I am sending you prophets and wise men and teachers of religious law. But you will kill some by crucifixion, and you will flog others with whips in your synagogues, chasing them from city to city. As a result, you will be held responsible for the murder of all godly people of all time—from the murder of righteous Abel to the murder of Zechariah son of Berekiah, whom you killed in the Temple between the sanctuary and the altar. I tell you the *truth*, this judgment will fall on this very generation."

—MATTHEW 23:1–5, 7, 13–17, 23–36

Okay, take a visual breath. Rest your eyes for a second.

Done? Can we talk about this for just a moment? That is *gangster*! Jesus called out the hypocritical leaders, saying they'd answer for all the deaths of all the godly people, throughout all time, from the beginning of time—yeah, *that* Abel.

So, I have two reasons why religion doesn't work: (1) the look of it and (2) the sound of it.

Let's dig into both of these reasons in the next two chapters.

Scripture References

Amos 5:21–23
Matthew 23:1–36

Practical Matters

Do you have any daily religious proclivities? Would they be empty without a certain person or thing?

_____

_____

_____

_____

_____

_____

_____

_____

Ask God if you have any religiosity in your walk with Him. Is there
any practice you're holding onto simply because you *think* you
should do it, but God's just not in it? What does He want you to do
about that?

_____

_____

_____

_____

_____

_____

_____

_____

Notes

What is God saying to you?

_____

_____

_____

_____

_____

_____

_____

_____

_____

_____

_____

_____

_____

_____

_____

_____

_____

_____

_____

seven

THE LOOK OF IT

*L*et's revisit a few verses from the passage in Matthew 23 really quickly:

> So practice and obey whatever they tell you, but don't follow their example. For they don't practice what they teach. They crush people with unbearable religious demands and never lift a finger to ease the burden.
>
> Everything they do is for show. . . . They love to receive respectful greetings as they walk in the marketplaces, and to be called "Rabbi."
>
> —VERSES 3–5, 7

The number one reason religion doesn't work is the look of it. Why? Because it doesn't look like Jesus.

I'm not talking about the liturgy of the church or a choir robe if that's the tradition you were raised in. It's not about a suit and tie.

None of that indicates whether you're operating in a religious spirit. It's the heart behind what you're doing that indicates whether you have a religious spirit or not. Because that's what Jesus is saying in the most scathing way: without the right heart, it doesn't work.

If you're walking around and everything you do is just for show, your heart is far from Him. If you're going to church just to see if anyone's looking, you have the wrong motive for coming to church. If the reason why you bought a certain outfit is because of the compliments at church, you are showing up for the wrong reasons. If you have a certain title or distinction that you *must* go by, then you care more about your verb than your noun. You're more focused on getting to the penthouse than being in the right place— where He is.

SPIRITUAL SUIT AND TIE

Short grammar break: When you care more about your verb, you're more invested in what you *do* than in who and Whose you are and who you do it for. Who you are is your noun.

This is why, when I was a lead pastor at Embassy City Church, we called members of the church "residents," and I would tell every resident, "Call me Tim." Because that's my *name*. "Pastor" is my verb. It's what I do. "Pastor Tim," therefore, is redundant if you already know I'm a pastor. Who are you reminding? *I* already know. *You* already know.

So Tim is fine.

If I were like Usain Bolt—which I'm not—and I dominated the sport of track and field for three different Olympic seasons and came home with nine gold medals, you wouldn't refer to me as

When you care more about your verb, you're more invested in what you do than in who and Whose you are and who you do it for. Who you are is your noun.

"Sprinter Tim." You would not call me the thing I did. You would call me who I am.

In the book of Acts there are seven sons of a man named Sceva. (Some people pronounce his name "Skeeva," but to me that sounds like a disease. So I smooth it over and say, "Si-vah.") Sceva's sons were really influenced and encouraged by Paul's ministry (Acts 19:13–22). They decided to go out and start doing what Paul did and preach in the name of Paul's God. Never mind that they should probably have had an encounter with that God themselves.

When they came upon a demon-possessed man, they said, "In the name of the God that Paul preaches about, come out of that man!"

They were talking to a demon!

Can you imagine the look the demon must have given those boys? The *double take*?

"Who, me? I mean, it looks like all seven fingers are pointing at me. I just wanted to make sure y'all were talking to me."

Well, this demon says to them, "Apostles I know, and prophets I know, and evangelists I know, but who are you?"

Wait . . . that's not what the demon said, is it?

Nope. He turned on the seven sons of Sceva and said, "I know Jesus, and I know Paul, but who are you?" (Acts 19:15). The possessed man jumped the sons of Sceva and did them *so* dirty—beat them up physically—that they fled from the scene "naked and battered" (verse 16).

Demons don't care about titles or your access to the penthouse suite. You can call yourself the apostle prophet evangelist of the second high pastoral teaching of the second *déspirit* jurisdictional regional bishop of the most high to the third corner of Tennessee, but if you don't have an actual relationship with Jesus, you will get *beat up*.

When I say the demon-possessed man beat up the sons of Sceva,

I mean they got the figurative, spiritual, and literal crap kicked out of them because religion doesn't work—not without Jesus.

CARNIVAL MIRROR

If it's the look of it that you think will bring you into a special relationship with God, you have severely disconnected yourself from the Christ who came to redeem us from the law that these religious people were talking about. Paul talked about this in his letter to the Philippian believers:

> Don't be selfish; don't try to impress others. Be humble, thinking of others as better than yourselves. Don't look out only for your own interests, but take an interest in others, too. You must have the same attitude that Christ Jesus had.
>
> —PHILIPPIANS 2:3–5

What Paul describes is the antithesis of a religious spirit. But the Pharisees wanted to put themselves in positions of honor where they could be looked at as "very, very important." (Feel free to imagine the air quotes I'm *liberally* applying here.)

To this day, many observant Jews wear boxes called *tefillin* on their wrists—and some even on their heads—with scriptures inside. It's based on a very literal interpretation of a few Old Testament passages. Before the Israelites entered the promised land, God told them,

> Fix these words of mine in your hearts and minds; tie them as symbols on your hands and bind them on your foreheads.
>
> —DEUTERONOMY 11:18 NIV

If you have an outward religious practice or symbol, but no real connection with Jesus and no real love for His Word, what's the point?!

Now, no disrespect to the *heart* behind this tradition. There's something beautifully interesting about a practice that symbolizes God's command to hold His words as close as possible to your mind or your body. But if that outward expression isn't matched by a heart and mind that actually loves and understands those words, the religious practice by itself isn't worth *squat*. Like a funhouse mirror, something doesn't *quite* add up.

I know this is going to hurt someone's feelings, but I have tattoos. They're great, but if I *have* to write all the scriptures that mean something to me on my body to feel closer to Him, is that relationship even real? If you have tattoos and they truly *mean* something to you, that's fine—I'm obviously not against tattoos! But what is the purpose behind it, really? Because Jesus isn't up in heaven saying, "*Sweet*, they'll remember the Word now that it's on their wrist! On their thigh! On their back!" Which, you're going to need a mirror for that—actually, you'll need two for the reflection. All I'm driving at is this: if you have an outward religious practice or symbol, but no real connection with Jesus and no real love for His Word, what's the point?!

ABOVE ALL

Okay, back to Paul's letter to the church in Philippi.

You must have the same attitude that Christ Jesus had.

> Though he was God,
> > he did not think of equality with God
> > as something to cling to.
> Instead, he gave up his divine privileges;

he took the humble position of a slave
and was born as a human being.
When he appeared in human form,
he humbled himself in obedience to God
and died a criminal's death on a cross.
Therefore, God elevated him to the place of highest
honor
and gave him the name above all other names,
that at the name of Jesus every knee should bow,
in heaven and on earth and under the earth,
and every tongue declare that Jesus Christ is Lord,
to the glory of God the Father.

—PHILIPPIANS 2:5–11

This is why God doesn't like the look of religion. He gave Jesus the *name* above all names, not a title. We know that He's Wonderful Counselor, Prince of Peace, Mighty God, the government's on His shoulders, *El Shaddai*, God is more than enough, *El Rophe*, all of it. We know He's the embodiment of all of that, but the scripture says He was given the "name that is above all other names."

Demons are not going to bow because you say, "In the name of the Savior, in the name of the crucified, in the name of the Christ anointed . . ." No, it's at His *name* that demons tremble, angels bow in reverence, and everyone on earth will too.

Why does God hate the look? Because it looks nothing like Him. Real transformative faith isn't a costume party. It would be like wearing a wedding dress but you have no groom, you're not even dating anyone—you're just *playing* at getting married!

It would be like standing in that penthouse party acting like you know Him and pantomiming for others what it means to know

Him, and all the while you're carrying something from those chargers filled with sin.

Do you realize that for every ceremonial robe the high priests put on, if Christ were to walk around in His own "ceremonial robes," transfigured as He was on Mount Tabor (Matthew 17), He would have blinded His entire city?

But Jesus Christ, our Savior, the Son of God, looked so regular, so different from the movie Jesus that you've seen on screen that Judas had to kiss Him on the cheek to identify Him. Jesus blended in so well with His other disciples that if Judas had kissed Peter, the guards would have gone, "Okay, take him, must be Jesus." *Insert shrug here.*

He wasn't in gleaming white robes while everyone else was in subdued hues to make Him look better. He never stepped out in His robes for the day and pointed at Peter like, "Peter, I'm going to need you to change that outfit. It's a bit too white. People will confuse my holiness with your sinful nature. Go with beige. Maybe taupe . . . I'll even take eggshell. Just not gleaming white."

Jesus was *so* regular He went to dinner with people that the religious people would never have gone to dinner with. He knew what was in those sinful people's hearts, and it was more pure than what the Pharisees were sporting. He knew it wasn't about what they had on. It was about what they had in their hearts.

Scripture References

Matthew 23:3–7
Acts 19:13–22
Philippians 2:3–11
Deuteronomy 11:18

Practical Matters

Let's dig deep for a moment. Do you care more about what you do (your vocation, your ministry, your serving and volunteering) than who (and Whose) you are?

_____

_____

_____

_____

_____

_____

Take a moment and ask God to help you see yourself the way He sees you and let go of the trappings of what it means to "be" your vocation.

_____

_____

_____

_____

_____

_____

_____

Notes

What is God saying to you?

_____

_____

_____

_____

_____

_____

_____

_____

_____

_____

_____

_____

_____

_____

_____

_____

_____

_____

eight

THE SOUND OF IT

Here's what was so corrupt and what so frustrated Jesus about the religious teachers—the teaching they gave placed incredibly harsh restrictions on people who were trying to do their best to live for God.

> "What sorrow awaits you teachers of religious law and you Pharisees. Hypocrites! For you shut the door of the Kingdom of Heaven in people's faces. You won't go in yourselves, and you don't let others enter either."
>
> —Matthew 23:13

Jesus was trying to make a point: the Law doesn't need a bunch of extra rules added to it. God left us the Ten Commandments, and we have more than enough work on our hands trying to obey those. I don't think you need to add 613 other commandments. But that's how many extra rules the Pharisees piled on top of the Law, covering petty little details from when we should wash to when we should go out to when we should step back. *That's* the core of Jesus' problem with the Pharisees—the hypocrisy.

I want you to have the correct context of hypocrisy, though. When we think about hypocrisy, we often think of somebody that's two-faced, maybe because that's the definition from the Greek. Hypocrisy under that definition means I see one face, but you've put another face behind that face. This is not the type of hypocrisy that Jesus was talking about.

> In English, hypocrisy describes a contradiction between reality and appearance. But in biblical usage, hypocrisy is misperceiving God's will, leading people astray, and thus incurring God's judgment. *Coupled with this is often a desire for prestige and power, abuse of teaching authority, false teachings on doctrine or practice, and preoccupation with ethical minutiae.* An accurate English term for this combination of factors is heresy.[1]

Does that emphasized part sound familiar at all?

What about these examples of some downright petty rules you might have encountered in your various church traditions?

- Sports events (baseball, football, fill in the blank) are evil because they're worldly.
- If you wear a beard, you're going to hell.
- If you read fiction or watch television shows, it's a sinful waste of time—some more than others.
- You have to wear white (or a suit or a tie, or whatever) when you come into the church.
- You better be here at every service we have—the Sunday

morning service, the Sunday evening service, the Tuesday Bible study service, the Wednesday main Bible Study service, the Thursday preparing for Sunday service meeting. If you miss any of those services, you may not be right with God.

Ever experienced a little bit of "ethical minutiae" in your history with the church? A little bit of pharisaical fanaticism?

Have you ever had a conversation at church that sounded something like this? "Hey, I was watching Netflix—"

The person you're talking with shudders like someone tripped over their grave.

You try again. "I saw this superhero show, *Daredevil*—"

Insert a melodramatic gasp here, maybe even the sign of the cross. "Don't watch TV! That's the one-eyed demon!"

A third of the people reading this just had one whole nightmare of a flashback.

Now, there are things that are just plain sins, and I don't need to go through a list of those things here. The problem is the unbearable regulations on top of what we're actually supposed to be getting convicted about by the Holy Spirit. Here's what I believe: I believe the Holy Spirit convicts people of sin, so we don't need to put together an impossibly long list of every *teeny tiny* way anyone might sin and hold that list of rules over everyone else's heads.

I teach against sin. I teach that we should live a life that is worthy of what Jesus did on the cross. But I also believe that the Holy Spirit is the main person—because Scripture says so—who convicts people of their sins. That's why coming to church every weekend to get a list of what not to do sounds so unnatural and strange and turns people off.

Do you know what a lot of people say about church? Or wonder

I believe the Holy Spirit convicts people of sin, so we don't need to put together an impossibly long list of every teeny tiny way anyone might sin.

why every church in America doesn't have fifty thousand people in it? "It's just a bunch of rules and regulations." You know what? They're not wrong. They're responding to the religious rules in so many churches that put so much *extra* on everyone's to-do list on top of actually living a life for Jesus Christ. But that's not our job as Christians.

You can sum up the whole of Jesus' criticism against the Pharisees like this: "The sound of that is not appealing to anybody, and it does not work."

Here's what happens when you build up a bunch of religious rules and give them deciding power over others' salvation: the people you want in the kingdom never actually come into the kingdom. They never end up in the Basement. They just wind up coming into your castle—most likely to the penthouse.

Let me be clear: I'm not coming against anybody's denomination, upbringing, or whatever. But if you've been under empty religious rules, you probably never made it to the kingdom. You just made it through your denomination's front door to their penthouse. And then it gets cultlike because if you don't do it "this way," you don't really have "it." You might even get kicked out.

Now I'm *really* talking to someone.

FAST FOOD BELIEF

I visited a church when I'd been saved something like ninety days. This church believed you weren't saved unless you spoke in tongues. Well, when I got saved, I didn't have a prayer language at first. So I went to this Bible study—because when you first get saved, your appetite opens up, and you just want to devour everything.

But sometimes you've got to check your plate. Check the chef, check the plate.

It might look like chicken, but where'd it come from? The same place McDonald's gets its chickens? Because if so, this is less like actual chicken and more like chicken and Silly Putty mixed together, and it might stay in my system for seven years.

Hold on—it might *stay in my system*.

If it's good food, it'll do all the nourishing of my body that it needs to and then come straight out. If it's bad food, it'll get in just as easily, but it'll be hard to get out.

The same is true spiritually. This is why people leave the church: because they can't get the bad food out of their system. They wind up with a grudge and go on a fast from the truth because they didn't realize they were eating dog food.

So I go to this church, and the guy leading the study says that if I'm not speaking in tongues, I'm not saved. I hadn't spoken in tongues yet, but I knew I was saved because I'd been convicted of all my sins. There was no half-Jesus experience for me. I was *fully* convicted.

One guy got up kind of sheepishly and said, "Well, I've never heard my grandmother speak in tongues, and she's a devout woman of God."

And the leader just said, "Oh, well . . ." and threw his hands in the air as if to imply, *Well, there it is. She doesn't have "it" yet.*

I came home to my mommy with my questions because that's what I do. I got saved and gave my life to Christ in my parents' church, God's Way Holiness Fellowship, on January 14, 1996. After I got saved, my mom would be in her bed, and I would love to come home and just lay my head on her lap and ask her questions about the Bible.

So I asked her about this experience. "Do I have to speak in tongues to be saved?" had barely come out of my mouth and my mom immediately went, "Hmm, that's not the truth at all. Baby, you got saved the moment you gave your life to Jesus. Whether you speak in tongues or not, you have a relationship with Jesus, and that person lied to you. Do not believe anything they said."

I said, "Okay!" and went on about my business.

Six months later I was by myself when I had a personal encounter with the Holy Spirit and I spoke in tongues. No prayer revival. No fancy church service. I very matter-of-factly had a prayer language. It was amazing and fantastic. No jumping through religious hoops necessary. It was done.

Here's what I want you to understand: Jesus wants to free everybody from the religious trappings of a to-do list. There is a discipleship process, and there are things that are in place to help you grow as a believer, but if you're really giving your life to Jesus, you will hunger for and *want* those things. You won't need anyone else to create laws to bind you to what *they* think you should do.

Let me prove it.

Then Jesus said, "Come to me, all of you who are weary and carry heavy burdens, and I will give you rest. Take my yoke upon you. Let me teach you, because I am humble and gentle at heart, and you will find rest for your souls. For my yoke is easy to bear, and the burden I give you is light."

—MATTHEW 11:28–30

Let me give you the context of what Jesus was talking about the way it might sound if He were standing in front of you today. "All of you who are bound to the religious laws of the religious, come to Me because you've been carrying a heavy burden. If you're trying to adhere to the Mosaic law and the 613 other laws that you've read about, come to Me. I know you've been surrounded by all that religious rulemaking. If you just come straight to Me, it'll be so light."

You'll be wondering, "I thought it was more than this. Are you sure that we're done?"

And He'll just smile and say, "Oh, we're done. That's all you have to do."

AND THAT WAS THAT

A few years back, my father-in-law was very, very sick. He hated God. If you listened to or watched a religious program in his home, he would start swearing and throwing things. My wife gave her life to Christ at the age of nine and began praying for her father from that moment till the man was seventy-three years old and on his deathbed. Twelve hours before he died, I had the opportunity to lead him to Christ.

Let me tell you how it happened.

There is this death rattle of labored breathing—once you've heard it, you'll never forget it—and that sound filled his bedroom. My father-in-law was lying in bed. His organs were shutting down. They'd told me he'd been nervous and fidgety the past few days, and he hadn't slept.

You know me—I walked into the room and just went, "Dad!" The man is on his deathbed, and I've just flown to Jamaica to see him, just as bright and loud as ever.

"Wha gwaan, man?"

"I came to see you!"

He leaned up in bed and fervently said, "I need you to pray for me." Exhausted, he slumped back down.

If you're trying to adhere to the Mosaic law and the 613 other laws that you've read about, come to Me.

I sat on the edge of the bed and said, "Well, Dad, that's what I came here for."

So I grabbed his hand, and I said a prayer for him. All the fidgeting they told me he'd been doing for the last forty-eight hours ceased. And he went to sleep—actual sleep, not death—but he was still holding my hand. I was trying to be sensitive and ease my hand out because, you know, he was *sleeping*, but every time I tried to move my hand, he'd wake up and look at me, shaking his head like, *Uh uh, don't do that.*

I'd been sitting there for about forty-five minutes when the Holy Spirit said, "Get your Bible and read him Romans 10:9."

Of course, I did it.

If you confess with your mouth that Jesus is Lord and believe in your heart that God raised him from the dead, you will be saved.

—ROMANS 10:9 ESV

I said, "Dad, do you believe that?"

He leaned up in his bed and said, "I do!"

"Well, you're saved."

And he leaned back into his bed and just kept nodding his head in affirmation like, *That's all I have to do? That's it, now?*

But here's what that looks like when you're dealing with religion: "Repeat after me. Dear Lord—"

"Dear Lord—"

"I believe—"

"I believe—"

Where did the sinner's prayer come from? What verse of the Bible? What translation?

Look, I don't have a problem with the sinner's prayer. What I'm saying is that when there's a man on his deathbed that can hardly talk, you mean to tell me I need to physically hear him go through the verbal back-and-forth to make sure he's saved?

"He died on a cross—"

"He died on a cross—"

"For my sins—"

"For my sins—"

"I believe—"

"I believe—"

"He was born of a virgin—"

". . . born of a virgin—Is this over yet? I'm almost dead!"

"Nope, gotta get you to the end of this. We've got three more paragraphs left here. Come on. You won't get into heaven without the sinner's prayer!"

Nope. I read him the scripture. He affirmed that he believed it. Twelve hours after that, he was in the presence of his Father.

Now, some of you reading this might still have a bit of a religious spirit thinking, *Nope. I don't think that cuts it.*

Let me make it just a little clearer for you.

Later that same year, I got hired at Gateway Church in Southlake, Texas. They invited Juliette and me to be part of their prophetic presbytery night.

If you've never heard of prophetic presbytery, in my experience it's when two or three people who have a gift of knowledge and the gift of prophecy from God come up and speak encouraging words into your life. Well, two of the presbyters had come up and said, "Hey Tim, is your dad here?" I said yes and pointed to him. One asked about my mom, and we pointed to her. They asked about my mother-in-law, and we pointed her out. Two of the three presbyters had acknowledged three out of our four parents.

The last presbyter comes up, walks straight up to Juliette, and says, "Hey Juliette. I know there's been something said about Tim's mom and dad and your mom, but last night, when I was in prayer, the Holy Spirit told me that your father is pleased with you."

Booyah.

Now, we don't have the space here for me to go into the complete theological context for this—that would be a whole book on its own—but in short, there's no one down in hell communicating and coming back to give us a handy heads-up that they're proud. And just so you know, God is the God of the *living*, not the dead. When He says He's the God of Abraham, Isaac, and Jacob, it's because those guys are *with* Him, still alive *with* Him, eternally *with* Him.

He's not talking about *dead* guys.

The presbyter said, "Your father *is* pleased with you."

Present tense. For my nongrammar nerds, that means *right now. Today.*

Juliette's dad is in heaven eternally. Twelve hours before he died, he received Christ in the most nonreligious way possible because Jesus' yoke is easy and His burden is light. When somebody wants to give their life to Jesus, you don't have to worry about all the *stuff.*

"Well, I still have a joint in my pocket, and I'm still going to get drunk tonight . . ."

Okay. Let me tell you another story.

FORGET THE PURGE PARTY

Two years before he died, my younger brother was drinking a forty-ounce beer. He was halfway done when the Holy Spirit convicted him of his sins, and he thought, *I need to get saved.* He got ready to call our dad.

At the same time, the Holy Spirit told my father, who was working the night shift at the post office and always left his phone in his car (because everyone was asleep), to go get his phone. He asked the Holy Spirit, "Why do You want me to go get my phone?"

"Go get the phone."

Can I just say that I love the way the Holy Spirit doesn't mince words with us sometimes? Just like a good parent.

Anyway, Dad went and got his phone. No sooner did he turn it on than it rang. It was my brother. My mind is blown by this.

"Dad, I need to give my life to Jesus. Do I have to wait until Sunday?"

Religion's in there. Do you see it?

My dad replied, "No, you don't have to wait until Sunday. If you confess with your mouth and believe in your heart that Jesus Christ is Lord, you'll be saved." There's Romans 10:9 again because it really is that simple.

My brother said, "Oh yeah, that's right." Like he'd just suddenly remembered. "Oh, well, thank you, Dad." He hung up the phone, gave his life to Jesus, and finished his beer.

Again, *booyah*.

It's hilarious.

Here's the thing—religion says, "Pour that beer out. Pour out the other forties you have. I want to see you tomorrow, and we're going to have a purge party! I'm going to get you on the altar and get you sober with the laying on of hands and with some oil. And *then* we can talk about whether you're saved."

But the Holy Spirit—who raised Jesus from the dead and operates in contradiction to our most religious habits—lets us know with this that He can *probably* handle some alcohol.

Scripture References

Matthew 23:13, 15
Matthew 11:28–30
Romans 10:9

Practical Matters

I'm going to ask you this question again because this is a safe space: Have you ever encountered someone with "a desire for prestige and power, abuse of teaching authority, false teachings on doctrine or practice, and preoccupation with ethical minutiae"? Maybe within a church environment? Maybe they even made you feel like you weren't saved unless you did something or experienced something specific?

Rest assured—this moment right here? This is a safe space for you. If you've ever encountered a moment in the body of Christ that hurt you or made you question if God was even there, I want to tell you right now, people are fallible. God is not. Bring that hurtful moment to Him now.

What does He want to tell you about it?

_____

_____

_____

_____

_____

Notes

What is God saying to you?

_____

_____

_____

_____

_____

_____

_____

_____

_____

_____

_____

_____

_____

_____

_____

_____

_____

_____

_____

_____

nine

WHAT SHOULD WE DO
WITH RELIGION?

Based on the fact that God doesn't like the look of it or the sound of it, what should we do with religion?

Get rid of it.

Don't misunderstand why I have come. I did not come to abolish the law of Moses or the writings of the prophets. No, *I came to accomplish their purpose*. I tell you the truth, until heaven and earth disappear, not even the smallest detail of God's law will disappear until its purpose is achieved. So if you ignore the least commandment and teach others to do the same, you will be called the least in the Kingdom of Heaven. But anyone who obeys God's laws and teaches them will be called great in the Kingdom of Heaven. But I warn you—unless your righteousness is better than the righteousness of the teachers of religious

Any law anyone is trying to hold or uphold outside of the context of Jesus Christ's life and teaching will lead to a religious spirit.

law and the Pharisees, you will never enter the Kingdom of Heaven!

—MATTHEW 5:17–20

Jesus said those words. Here's what they mean: any law anyone is trying to hold or uphold outside of the context of Jesus Christ's life and teaching will lead to a religious spirit.

Did you catch that?

Any law.

All the law of Moses can be completely summed up in Jesus' life. He taught it more than once: "You've heard it said . . . but I have come to tell you . . ."

The law of Moses was all external. "Do this, *don't* do that."

But Jesus was saying that He isn't trying to change our behavior—He's trying to change our *hearts*. Because if He can change your heart, that will change your mind. If He can change your mind, that will lead to changed behavior. There don't need to be any rules and regulations to try to keep you in place. Newsflash: the rules and regulations *never* actually worked.

IT'S ALL ABOUT YOUR HEART

In our current culture of Christianity, I'm extremely grateful for churches that build a community of people that have the *desire* to please God, as opposed to being *forced* to please God.

In our residency classes at Embassy City Church (remember, "residents" is what we called members), we said something that kind of freaked people out: "If you're going to be a resident of our church, cool! Come to church . . . but don't be here every week."

People would just stare at us.

The point is we *want* you to go on vacation. You don't have to plan your family's summer vacation between Sundays. That's a religious spirit. There's no need to leave on Monday and be back by Saturday to be "counted in the kingdom." You were counted in the kingdom when you gave your life to Jesus.

I wasn't even there every Sunday when I was the lead pastor! I was *going* on vacation! I already had a guest speaker lined up because *I wasn't going to be there.*

And this isn't *just* about going to church. Think about it. You can choose to walk into an office unimpeded or fight your way into a title or a position. Believe me, I understand fighting for something that you've worked so hard for. But at the end of the day, if God has not *called* you to that position, to that title, then you don't have the grace for it. *Period.* You're doing it without Him.

If you want it—whatever *it* is (a marriage, a job, an opportunity)—and you fight hard enough for it, you might actually get it. But you may not actually *want* what you get at the end of it.

God put it this way, through the prophet Amos:

> What sorrow awaits you who say,
>> "If only the day of the LORD were here!"
> You have no idea what you are wishing for.
>> That day will bring darkness, not light.
> In that day you will be like a man who runs from
>> a lion—
>> only to meet a bear.
> Escaping from the bear, he leans his hand against a
>> wall in his house—
>> and he's bitten by a snake.

Yes, the day of the LORD will be dark and hopeless,
>   without a ray of joy or hope.
"I hate all your show and pretense—
>   the hypocrisy of your religious festivals and
>>   solemn assemblies.
I will not accept your burnt offerings and grain
>   offerings.
>   I won't even notice all your choice peace
>>   offerings.
Away with your noisy hymns of praise!
>   I will not listen to the music of your harps.
Instead, I want to see a mighty flood of justice,
>   *an endless river of righteous living.*

"Was it to me you were bringing sacrifices and offerings during the forty years in the wilderness, Israel? No, you served your pagan gods—Sakkuth your king god and Kaiwan your star god—the images you made for yourselves. So I will send you into exile, to a land east of Damascus," says the LORD, whose name is the God of Heaven's Armies.

—AMOS 5:18–27

That's *gangster*, right? Old Testament God spit such game that after He was done speaking, your response couldn't be anything but, "You know what? I think I'm just going to take myself to my room, okay?"

Sidenote: that italicized line, "an endless river of righteous living"? That's where Martin Luther King Jr. got that line from. It's a quote he read to the nation, and it's now on display in the National Museum of African American History and Culture. Sorry, I'm done nerding out. Back to the subject . . .

Could we make it in the world of the Old Testament today? No, I don't think we could. Nobody could. The law is, and always has been, beyond any human's ability to obey perfectly.

Thankfully we're under a different dispensation today—because of God's grace and Jesus' sacrifice, we're not going to get penalized the way we would have back then—but God still wants an Old Testament *reverence* from us because, without that understanding, you cannot appreciate what Christ did on the cross.

UNWORTHY SACRIFICES

Okay, I have a little homework for you.

Homework?

Yes. Nerds rule the world, remember?

Go read Isaiah 1:2–20. Do you hear what God is saying? He's basically asking the people, "What makes you think I *want* all your sacrifices?" Remember, He instituted these things! The sacrifices, the Sabbath, the festivals—He instituted them *all* to bring people closer to Him, but in this passage He is tangibly disgusted by those acts. Why? Because over time the people forgot to include Him. They got wrapped up in the *doing* and started observing the sacrifices, the Sabbath, and the festivals without Him. And it all became nothing but a burden.

I'm thinking about a few different churches when I read the passage in Isaiah. Who told you to parade through town like that? Who told you to host this conference? God did not ask for all that pomp and circumstance. It's like a man ignoring his wife all year and then showing up on Valentine's Day with a dozen roses. She didn't ask for roses—she asked for *you*.

My oldest son, Nathan, was thirteen when he celebrated his first Valentine's Day with a "real" Valentine Like. (He didn't get to have a Valentine's Love yet because he was too young for all that, so he got a Valentine's Like.)

As he was planning to get something for her, he came and asked me, "Dad, are you getting Mom anything for Valentine's Day?"

I calmly said, "No. Your mother and I have not gotten anything for each other for Valentine's Day since we've been married. For us, every day is Valentine's Day. Your mom and I get stuff all throughout the year. If we only had this day to highlight, that means I haven't paid attention to her the way I should for the whole year."

He nodded at me. "Yeah, that makes sense."

Right?!

I DON'T WANT YOUR BAND-AID

Okay, walk with me here because I'm about to go deep and get *really* pointed.

The events of 2020 came. George Floyd was murdered, gasping for his mom. Breonna Taylor was killed in her own apartment. Ahmaud Arbery got his guts blown out on his daily jog. And—all of a sudden—everyone wants to celebrate Black History Month like it's something *new*? That's not what we asked for. We didn't ask for you to put "Black Lives Matter" on the basketball court or acknowledge a few Black people after the Super Bowl. What we asked for was *equality*.

In the same way, all that—the pomp and circumstance, the baseless actions all without God, without the actual purpose behind it all—all that does is put a Band-Aid on a gushing relational wound.

As a culture, we have thoroughly murdered the sacred cow—cut it up and burned it on the altar of people's expectations. But God is saying, "Come back. I want your heart."

As a culture, we have thoroughly murdered the sacred cow—cut it up and burned it on the altar of people's expectations. But God is saying, "Come back. I want your *heart*."

Scripture References

Matthew 5:17–20
Amos 5:18–27
Isaiah 1:2–20

Practical Matters

Real talk (and no shame): Take a moment and ask God if there are any acts in your journey with Him that you're just doing by rote or because you feel it's expected of you. A Lord's Prayer recited just for the sake of saying it does nothing, but with your heart fully turned toward God, it'll shake mountains.

Have you gotten wrapped up in any "doing"? Have you gotten so into the habit of doing something that you've begun to leave God out of it?

_____

_____

_____

_____

_____

_____

Notes

What is God saying to you?

_____

_____

_____

_____

_____

_____

_____

_____

_____

_____

_____

_____

_____

_____

_____

_____

_____

_____

part Three

IDENTIFYING UPSETTERS

Ten

WHO ARE
"THOSE PEOPLE"?

*D*id you die? Nope, still breathing? Still reading? Okay, good!

But are you upset?

Because if you're going to be a Basement Dweller who has had their life turned upside down by Jesus Christ, you're going to live an upset life. That life comes with a mandate to invite other people to the Basement. That means *you* will be an upsetter.

This is going to be a *really* short chapter because I'm about to make it *really* simple.

What do I mean by "upsetter"? Let me give you a definition.

Upsetter (n.): Someone who has been upset and upsets others.

An upsetter in the kingdom of God is a person who has been upset by the power and transformative work of God, Jesus Christ, and the Holy Spirit, and then they go out and upset others.

An upsetter in the kingdom of God is a person who has been upset by the power and transformative work of God, Jesus Christ, and the Holy Spirit, and then they go out and upset others.

The only way to truly define Basement Dwellers is to find not only someone whose life has been upset but who is also willing to go out and upset the lives of others with the message of the power and love of Jesus Christ.

Again, I'm not using the word "upset" to talk about someone feeling angry.

Although if you are someone who adheres to the biblical precepts, laws, commands, decrees, and instructions in the Word of God, you are bound to upset someone who doesn't share that same belief system.

By definition, upsetters have five qualities or attributes that are indigenous to who they are when they come into a relationship with Jesus Christ. If someone is going to lead an upset life and upset others, they have to have these five things. If they don't, then I'm not sure they're upsetting correctly and I'm not sure if anyone they talk to is actually on their way to the Basement.

Upsetters must . . .

1. love Jesus,
2. love people,
3. be Spirit-filled,
4. do good, and
5. love life.

Let me break those five essentials down for you in the following chapters.

Practical Matters

Take a moment and ask God how He feels about how you talk to people about Him.

_____

_____

_____

_____

_____

_____

_____

Notes

What is God saying to you?

_____

_____

_____

_____

_____

_____

eleven

UPSETTERS LOVE JESUS

Have you ever met *that* kind of believer? You know, the one jumping on couches with a face shining overwhelmingly bright with a forced glow? They're the type who *shout* into work on a Monday morning like, "I'm in love with *Jesus!*" Every time you see them and ask a simple, "Hey, how are you doing?" their response is something like, "Bless God! Highly favored of the Lord! I'm the head and not the tail! I'm above and not beneath! Got everything going on in Jesus' name!"

I just . . . all I did was ask how you are. We're at *work*. A simple good morning would suffice. I did not ask for a declaration of your faith—it's seven o'clock in the morning on a Monday. Turn it down!

When I say upsetters love Jesus, I'm not talking about the loud "overwhelm (and annoy) everyone around you" kind of love.

I'm talking about a love that is intimate. It's personal. It's deep. It's reverential. I'm talking about the kind of love that leads to faithfulness and fidelity in Jesus Christ. That makes you change the way you live because you've fallen in love with Jesus.

This isn't the cultural Christian Jesus. This isn't the love that requires a necklace with a cross on it, rhinestoned, bedazzled, sparkling in the visible shimmer of your faith. No one thinks you have faith specifically because you have a tattoo of Jesus creeping up the back of your arm.

The kind of love I'm talking about happens when you're all alone and there's no one else around. When there's a moment in the morning, afternoon, or evening when you *have* to spend time with Jesus. When everything else has stilled around you, or you even force all the noise and craziness to a screeching halt, and you say, "Enough. I *have* to spend some time with Jesus. I must be in His presence. I have to read His Word." You're in love with the person who saved your soul, made you whole, and turned your whole life upside down.

IRREVOCABLE CHANGE

Paul talks about that kind of love:

> Peace be with you, dear brothers and sisters, and may God the Father and the Lord Jesus Christ give you love with faithfulness. May God's grace be eternally upon all who love our Lord Jesus Christ.
>
> —EPHESIANS 6:23–24

There's no way you could do that on your own. Something has to have happened in your heart to cause you to change. Things you never would have been convicted of before, you're convicted of. Things you never would have been concerned about before, you're now concerned about.

The reason why an upsetter can't be an upsetter without loving Jesus is because only people who are in love are infectious.

You used to think going to church was crazy, and now you find yourself in there every weekend. You thought people who read the Bible were weird, and now you're reading yours every day.

Love does crazy things to you.

The reason why an upsetter can't be an upsetter without loving Jesus is because only people who are in love are infectious.

People only follow someone if they see that person is really passionate about something. People who aren't passionate don't have people following them. But if you're passionate about something, people will follow your passion.

Here's the thing about the kingdom that's so amazing, and it's the backbone of the Basement philosophy: it's that the whole thing is upside down. We fall in love with Jesus and become so passionate about following Him that it makes other people stare in wonder.

"How, though?" they ask. "You? *You* love Jesus?"

It makes them want to know where we're hanging out when we enter that elevator and press *B*.

I love the individuality of the redemptive power of Christ. Everyone that gives their life to Jesus has the opportunity to shock other people. When you're the kind of person who makes people say, "I can't imagine that *they* would ever give their life to Jesus"—but then you *do*? That makes an impact.

That makes people wonder how they can press *B* too.

MY NEW BEST FRIENDS

When I gave my life to Jesus, I was twenty years old. I was a local and regional performer—this was early in my rapping days—so my friends and I were in the club every single weekend. After service at my parents' church, we went straight to Venice Beach. After Venice Beach, we went out to eat at M&M's Soul Food or Roscoe's Chicken and Waffles. After Roscoe's, we'd cruise Crenshaw Boulevard until two or three in the morning. Wash, rinse, repeat.

January 14, 1996, was a Sunday that should have been like any other Sunday. I'd stayed out until about four or five in the morning clubbing, then took a nap and drove my parents to the church where my mom was the pastor.

We'd moved houses and cities but left the church where it was—sixty-six miles away from our new home—so my parents had a commute every weekend. Since I lived in their house and they were bivocational (they worked jobs all week, then led the church on the weekend), I figured I should probably help them out any way I could.

I walked in as Sunday school was wrapping up and they were getting ready to start worship. I sat in the back, ready to do what I normally did at every single service: laugh at the people who spoke in tongues, write raps, and generally not be engaged in the service.

They got maybe one song into the worship set and, clear as you're hearing my words to you now in your mind from the black ink on this white page, I heard the voice of the Holy Spirit in that moment.

"Tim, you're a sinner."

I know that sounds harsh on paper, but in that moment there was no condemnation in the Holy Spirit's voice. It was just like pointing out "there are flowers in your yard" when it's springtime or "the sky is blue" on a clear day. It was such a matter-of-fact statement.

If someone spilled mustard on their shirt, you would probably just say, "Hey, you got mustard on your shirt." You wouldn't point with all the aggression of a fire-and-brimstone preacher and shout, "YOU GOT MUSTARD ON YOUR SHIRT!"

The Holy Spirit doesn't do that either.

The moment He pointed that out, it was the first time I realized I was disconnected from a relationship with God. I literally just *didn't* have a relationship with Him at all—and I *needed* it! For the first time, I was convicted of my sin and the way I'd been living.

I knew I had to give my life to Christ right then and there. Problem? It was a Pentecostal church. We'd only *just* started morning worship. There were at least three hours before the altar call. We were about to have A, B, C, D, and E worship selections. We were probably going to have a testimony service. There was the offering to raise. Then the sermon, and that would probably go as long as it went. Only *then* would we get to the altar call.

I just *knew* I was three hours away from salvation and eternal life. I couldn't wait that long!

My dad was officiating the service that day, and during the testimony service, the Holy Spirit told me to get up. My dad opened the floor for testimonies, and about five people got up in front of me. My dad habitually addressed the congregation from front to back, so I was the last to go.

When he got to me, he went, "Um . . . I think Tim has something to say?"

All I said was, "I give up."

Of course, no one knew what I meant, so I added, "I need to give my life to Jesus right now."

From the front row, my mom let out the biggest, loudest, Blackest "HALLELUJAH JESUS!" that you have ever heard in your life—it was *churchy*.

My dad was crying.

I started crying.

My Sunday school teacher, Beverly Walker, started crying.

I walked up to the front of the church and gave my life to Jesus. That was it.

No sermon preached.

No altar call given.

The Holy Spirit brought me to Jesus, and I gave my life to Him.

My friend Steven and my brother, Myles, came to pick me up after service—they had it timed perfectly. We were supposed to head to Venice. Myles had skipped church that morning, so he rode with them. When they got there, I gave Steven a hug and said, "What's up, man?" Then I hugged my brother.

Myles looked at me, and he just *knew*. He went, "Aw no you didn't . . . You did it, didn't you?"

I just said, "Yeah, I did."

"I respect that, man. I respect that." Then he kind of nodded to himself and went, "We'll see you later." He jumped in the car with our friend, and they went to Venice Beach.

NEW LIFE

Within twenty-four hours, my best friends were my parents, my Bible, and my PlayStation. Within twenty-four hours, everyone had left me completely alone. I don't see it as them disrespecting or abandoning me. Quite the contrary, actually. They *were* respecting the decision I made.

I fell in love, and the moment that I fell in love, things changed.

I immediately stopped going to the clubs. Admittedly, there were some things that didn't come off *as* immediately as that—but there was something that started changing on the inside of my heart and my mind that had me before God going, "Lord, I'm in love with

You. If that means I don't have a single friend, then I just want to pursue You."

Love will make you change.

If you've somehow come into a relationship with Jesus Christ and nothing about you has changed, I challenge you that you probably didn't mean it. It's that simple. We just talked in the last few chapters about religion. If you've never really met Him, I can see how you come into a set of rules and regulations and never actually change because it leaves you acting in *your* strength, *your* power, *your* will, and *your* way.

But when you fall in love with Jesus and you have your heart transformed, you're not relying on your will or your way anymore. You're relying on Someone else.

Scripture Reference

Ephesians 6:23–24

Practical Matters

When you talk to people about Jesus, are you focused on being "upset" according to the angry definition? Think of your tone and even the heart behind your words. Are you communicating fire and brimstone or are you extending a quiet invitation to the Basement?

_____

_____

_____

But when you fall in love with Jesus and you have your heart transformed, you're not relying on your will or your way anymore.

Are you determined to upset others for Christ and inspire them to turn their understanding of Him and the world upside down with His message?

_____

_____

_____

_____

_____

_____

Notes

What is God saying to you?

_____

_____

_____

_____

_____

_____

Twelve

UPSETTERS LOVE PEOPLE

*I*f you'll forgive me in advance, I'm about to poke at your previous understandings and conceptions of some things. Please keep all booing and hissing to a minimum and hear me out.

When you look at this chapter title, there is the automatic Christian response of "Absolutely, we love people! We're all about people! We might not love what they *do*, but we love *them*."

The following verses are in red in your Bible, so don't get mad at me for what you're about to read. If you want to get mad at someone, you need to get mad at *Jesucristo*. (Feel free to imagine me working on my accent and practicing my Spanish here—I absolutely am and I take every opportunity to do so.)

> "You have heard the law that says, 'Love your neighbor' and hate
> your enemy. But I say, love your enemies! Pray for those who
> persecute you! In that way, you will be acting as true children of
> your Father in heaven. For he gives his sunlight to both the evil

and the good, and he sends rain on the just and the unjust alike. If you love only those who love you, what reward is there for that? Even corrupt tax collectors do that much. If you are kind only to your friends, how are you different from anyone else? Even pagans do that. But you are to be perfect, even as your Father in heaven is perfect."

—Matthew 5:43–48

Upsetters love people. *All kinds* of people. *Everybody.* They even love people who *hate* them and *despise* them. Upsetters love people who most in the church might think are unlovable.

Liberal people.

Homosexual people.

Undocumented people.

All colors of people.

If I'm getting under your skin, remember to hold the hissing.

But if I'm not yet, let me poke just a little harder.

Maybe you do love all kinds of people and everyone loves you for it . . . but what about people who *don't* love you?

How do you love *them*?

We just talked about it in the last chapter. Go back if you need a refresher—you have to love Jesus to love people who don't love you.

I think this is crucial. If you are going to be a real upsetter and get as many people to the Basement as you can, you have to stop exclusively going after people and praying for people that are amicable to you. You have to start purposefully seeking out people that are a little bit obstinate. People who have no intention of hearing about this place and are a little bit rude to you when they tell you so. People who don't even want to talk to you.

Don't like you.

Upsetters love people. All kinds of people. Everybody. They even love people who hate them and despise them.

Got anger issues.

More than a little attitude.

THE AMBASSADORSHIP

Remember, you're an ambassador for Jesus Christ. You *get* to change the atmosphere around you. The way you do that is by taking on the mind of Jesus and saying, "I'm just going to love everyone the same way You did."

It doesn't mean you have to like what they're saying or doing, but you do have to love them. You have to die to your will and respond with the nature and character of Jesus.

That's what a quiet invitation is all about.

Can I give you an example?

Back when I lived in LA, my friend got me a temp position at a place that created advertisements and magazine ads, and there was a little lady who worked there. When I say little, I mean that without her heels, she *might* have been five feet tall—maybe.

You knew she was at work because whenever she came to the office, the sound of her steps preceded her.

THUMP, THUMP, THUMP, THUMP, THUMP.

I don't know if she put sound effects in her heels to give her steps that robust sound or what, but that's how she walked in every day.

THUMP, THUMP, THUMP, THUMP, THUMP.

Everyone knew the sound of her footsteps and everybody knew to steer clear and get *out* of her way.

Did I mention she was mean?

She was a clock-watcher. Micromanagerial in the *extreme*. If you went to lunch at one o'clock, you had better be back at your desk and in your seat by 1:59:59. She was just too much. Everyone was scared of her!

But I just didn't see why. I could see that underneath all of the stomping and micromanaging, she was sweet, and I said so. Everyone thought I was crazy! They didn't understand that I was looking way past what I could see with my eyes.

There were two or three other believers at work, and I suggested that we should just go after her.

They were like, "You mean we should jump her after work?"

"What? No. Redeem your flesh. No, I didn't mean we should beat her up." I told them we could go after her, and she wouldn't even know it. We could just start *praying for her*. We could start praying over the office and really start doing something in the atmosphere of our workplace. We decided to get there early over the next couple of days just to pray in the office, break up some spiritual stuff that was affecting the atmosphere, and see if it worked.

For about a week we got there early, and we'd walk around the office and pray. I started bringing some olive oil and dabbling it—not dabbling it like I'm dancing, but just dabbling a little of it on everyone's chairs. I didn't pour oil all over everything so people were wondering what in the world happened to their seats—though I did mess up one time: I stood up on the copy machine to dabble a little oil on the little lady's door. She had one of those *big* office doors, so I had to get up on the copy machine on my tippy toes to reach the top, and I put a little cross there with the oil. I don't know if the heat that close to the ceiling made it spread or what, but it just started dripping down. Thankfully, she didn't notice.

Anyway, we prayed around the office for a week. The following week, you want to know what happened?

Monday, she walks in . . .

THUMP, THUMP, THUMP, THUMP, THUMP.

Tuesday, she walks in . . .

THUMP, THUMP, THUMP, THUMP, THUMP.

Wednesday . . .

THUMP, THUMP, THUMP, THUMP, THUMP.

I know you're waiting impatiently for the breakthrough, but nope. She was *still* stomping.

Now, I don't know what happened between Wednesday and Thursday, but Thursday morning, she walked in . . .

Thump, thump, thump, thump, thump . . .

It was easing up. Unbelievable!

This was Friday:

. . . .

We didn't even know she'd gotten to work! No one heard *anything*, and that would have been breakthrough enough, right? No, no! She came out at lunch and said, "Anyone want pizza?"

She bought the *whole* office pizza.

She had the whole office looking at her like, "Who *are* you?"

Within three weeks, she'd started asking us to pray for her.

I left eventually—remember, it was just a temp position—but my friend who got me the job became good friends with her. They started going to Bible study together. She even started taking classes on her own.

You know why?

Because we decided to just start loving *everybody*.

BE THE LIGHT IN THE ROOM

It wasn't just the three of us believers in the office in a little Christian clique ignoring everyone else because they didn't love Jesus. Clutching

They won't see Him unless They see Him in you. And if you're too busy huddled in the corner ignoring them, they won't see Him in you.

our "Jesus first, then coffee" mugs in the corner, sneering and muttering, "They're just *different*. I can't *stand* them. God *save* them."

How's He going to do that if you never open your mouth to show them who He is? Who are you to deny them and shut them out when you're the very light they need to *see* Him? They won't see Him unless they see Him in you. And if you're too busy huddled in the corner ignoring them, they *won't* see Him in you.

This is one of the most racially charged, politically crazy seasons our country and our world have ever been in. People are mad at each other based on a single comment or post they see on Twitter, Facebook, and Instagram—even based on what a *bumper sticker* says.

You could be in traffic, see someone's bumper sticker, and immediately go, "I can't *stand* them!"

It's a bumper sticker. Why you mad?

Just love them.

Because if you don't, His kingdom can't come to them. They'll never see His love through your hate and they'll never make it to the Basement.

Scripture Reference

Matthew 5:43–48

Practical Matters

Do you find yourself struggling to invite people to the Basement who are different from you? Different background, different culture, different sex?

_____

_____

_____

_____

_____

_____

_____

_____

How do you feel about reaching out to people who don't like you or maybe have an attitude problem? In that environment, are there any other Christians you can partner with to pray for someone like that? (I feel like I should mention that the person you're praying for does _not_ need to know about it.)

_____

_____

_____

_____

_____

_____

_____

_____

Notes

What is God saying to you?

_____

_____

_____

_____

_____

_____

_____

_____

_____

_____

_____

_____

_____

_____

_____

_____

_____

_____

Thirteen

UPSETTERS ARE
SPIRIT-FILLED

I want to give you the most concise passage I can for being Spirit-filled without folding a whole separate book into the middle of this one—that just feels counterproductive.

> Don't be drunk with wine, because that will ruin your life. Instead, be filled with the Holy Spirit.
>
> —Ephesians 5:18

Boom. You can turn. Just don't turn *up.*

Look at the parallel. Of *all* the things to compare being filled with the Holy Spirit to, why use wine? Why wine as a comparative analysis of the person of the Holy Spirit?

Because alcohol has an effect on your body and spirit that is a counterfeit of what the Holy Spirit does.

TURNT

Have you ever seen a drunk person? Hold on, let's be transparent now. It's just you reading in a room by yourself, after all—I'm not even really there. Have you ever *been* drunk? Like *ridiculously* drunk? Woke up the next day with no recollection of what happened *drunk-drunk*?

Why would God say don't be drunk with wine, be drunk with the Holy Spirit? Because they both have the same effect: They both change your behavior. They both change the way you walk. They both change the way you talk.

When you remember that drunk person you saw (or recall that drunk moment with murky detail), there was a massive behavior change, right? Some call it liquid courage.

It's amazing to me how many people—even some traditions within Christianity—believe speaking in tongues is *so* taboo, but if you've ever listened to a drunk person try to talk, it's pretty close.

At Thanksgiving dinner, your drunk uncle is babbling, absolutely incoherent, but somehow still adamant that you listen and convinced that he makes perfect sense—*he don't*. But he's got a death grip on your arm, and you cannot escape.

Then an interpreter has to show up—usually your aunt—and clear up the message.

"What he meant to say was, 'Do you remember ten years ago, when we went on that RV trip, how much fun we had?'"

Wow. Speaking in tongues. Interpretation of tongues. This is in the Bible!

I led a Spirit-filled, Spirit-led church, and it's something I don't think should be taboo to talk about. There's God the Father, God the Son, and God the Holy Spirit.

You can't upset *anyone* without the Holy Spirit because He *is* the Upsetter.

> The Spirit of God, who raised Jesus from the dead, lives in you.
> —ROMANS 8:11

Okay, that's a simple sentence, but let's break it down.

The same Spirit that raised Christ Jesus from the dead.

Is Christ's resurrection the most upsetting thing that happened in all of human history? Yes, it is.

Who did it? The Holy Spirit.

He lives in you, so you have the ability to go upset others. If you don't have Him, you can't upset anybody, therefore you can't actually invite anyone to the Basement.

BREAK THE TABOO

Maybe you just don't get it every time someone talks about the Holy Spirit. Maybe you don't like the idea of not having control because "giving your life" to the Holy Spirit means you don't have the control you crave.

Yeah . . . you're going to have to get used to that if you're going to walk with Jesus.

A lot of people have more respect for hard spirits and liquor than they do for the Holy Spirit. But in the same way a drunk person is not in control—and the alcohol makes them do crazy stuff and say crazy things that make no sense—people who are Spirit-filled are also not in control, but they do *amazing* stuff and say *amazing* things because the Holy Spirit *is* in control.

You can't upset anyone without the Holy Spirit because He is the Upsetter.

This is why Paul's comparative analysis is so amusing to me. Because why do that cheap imitation? The Holy Spirit will do the *real* thing if you'll just let Him. He'll change your behavior. He'll change the way you walk. But you won't be stumbling around. You will walk upright, in a straight line, with integrity, character, and morals.

He'll change the way you talk too. And I'm not just talking about speaking in tongues! Everyone's so scared even at the *mention* of tongues, but allowing the Holy Spirit to upset you and instigate you to change will change the way you talk on a daily basis. It'll even change the stuff you talk about. It'll change your conversation. You won't want to gossip anymore. You won't want to spread rumors anymore.

Being around people changes you. Being in relationship with *anyone* changes you, and being in a relationship with the Holy Spirit is just like any other relationship that you have. Think about your relationships with the people you love the most. Your parents. Your siblings. Your spouse. Your best friends. How often do you talk to them?

Every week?

Every day?

Every hour? With technology these days, if you're in a really close relationship with someone, it's not impossible.

What I'm talking about is a deep level of intimacy that goes beyond even that. This isn't talking to your mom or your best friends—even if you do that every day. I'm talking about someone who lives with you—*in* you, 24 hours a day, 7 days a week, 365 days a year. You *always* have access to someone who can and will bring you peace, show you where to go, talk to you about anything and everything, help you process through every grief and disappointment, celebrate with you through every win and success, and give you *direct* access to the very presence of God.

Be confident and comfortable enough to have a conversation with *that* Holy Spirit. Even as comfortable as you are texting your friends in the middle of the night about the show you're bingeing on Netflix. Don't be scared of the Holy Spirit! He likes you . . . a lot. Enough to live on the *inside* of you.

I mean, you can live *in* a house with someone, but they don't live *in* you. The mere fact that the Holy Spirit would want to live *in* you—and you *know* how you can be! The fact that He wants that intimacy with you and is that patient with you, but you don't even want to talk to Him? Now that's just crazy.

If you don't come from the kind of faith background where talking to the Holy Spirit is normal, supported, or accepted—or maybe it's even *weird*—that's okay. You don't have to talk to Him *loudly*. You can whisper it. You can even just talk to Him in your head and in your heart—He lives in you. He will hear you.

You have no idea what it will do to your relationship with God and how much stronger that relationship will become if you just start having conversations with the Holy Spirit.

Not until you start.

Scripture References

Ephesians 5:18
Romans 8:11

You don't have to talk to Him loudly. You can whisper it. You can even just talk to Him in your head and in your heart— He lives in you. He will hear you.

Practical Matters

What does it look like to start having that conversation with the Holy Spirit? Let's get really practical: it's the same way you'd talk to a friend on the phone. We paralyze ourselves when we think our prayer life has to be this polished oratory experience. Stop, fam. This is more of a conversation than it is a speech. If you're tired today, tell Him. Ask for His energy, His strength. You don't have to wait to give a grandiose speech precipitated by problems—though we all face problems in life. Talking with the Holy Spirit is precipitated by communion. This is your *dad*. So pick up your spiritual phone and just call your daddy.

What does this look like?

_____

_____

_____

Where can you take time out of your schedule to spend time hearing the Holy Spirit?

_____

_____

_____

You won't recognize who you're talking to unless you know His voice. You have to read. Spend time in His presence, in His Word. Here are just a few extra places (beyond those already listed in the previous pages and those still to come) to start in Scripture, where you can begin to recognize God's voice through the Holy Spirit. I'm including scriptures from both the Old Testament and the New Testament because (1) the Psalms are arguably one of the best times the Holy Spirit spit bars through the authors of the Bible and (2) more importantly, I want you to see that the precedent has legs—we've *always* been able to hear His voice. We just have to get in His presence and listen.

Exodus 19:9

Numbers 7:89

Deuteronomy 4:12

Deuteronomy 5:23

Deuteronomy 28:1–2

1 Samuel 3:10

Job 33:14–15

Psalm 25:4–5

Psalm 37:7–9

Psalm 119:89

Psalm 119:105

Isaiah 6:8

Daniel 10:9

Luke 8:21

John 8:47

John 10:2–4

John 10:27–28

John 14:26

Acts 13:2–3

Romans 10:17

Titus 1:2

Hebrews 4:7

Revelation 3:20

Notes

What is God saying to you?

_____

_____

_____

_____

fourteen

UPSETTERS DO GOOD

*L*et me ask you a question: Who is our chief example? You can say it out loud, maybe mutter it under your breath if you're reading in a coffee shop or something. Or, you know, just shout right there in your local Starbucks. Your prerogative.

It's Jesus! Right!

> And you know that God anointed Jesus of Nazareth with the Holy Spirit and with power. Then Jesus went around *doing good and healing* all who were oppressed by the devil, for God was with him.
>
> —ACTS 10:38

We know that God anointed Jesus with the Holy Spirit and with power. So, it stands to reason that if Jesus had Him, we should have Him. If you don't believe me, look at John 14:15–18:

> If you love me, obey my commandments. And I will ask the Father, and he will give you another Advocate, who will never leave you. He

We know that God anointed Jesus with the Holy Spirit and with power. So, it stands to reason that if Jesus had Him, we should have Him.

is the Holy Spirit, who leads into all truth. The world cannot receive him, because it isn't looking for him and doesn't recognize him. But you know him, because he lives with you now and later will be in you. No, I will not abandon you as orphans—I will come to you.

It's right there in red ink, and it's simple, right?

Back to Acts 10:38.

I had a thought. Whether you have a church background or not, no matter what denomination you were raised in or what your theological persuasion is, most people lean one of two ways: There are the people that love simply doing good works in Jesus' name, like paying it forward in the Starbucks line or donating clothes to a shelter. Then there are people who *only* want to operate in the miraculous power of Jesus and do miracles like casting out demons and healing the oppressed.

But here's what I'm saying: do both.

Let's just keep it real simple. It's not either/or; it's both/and.

Jesus went around doing good *and* healing all those who were oppressed by the devil.

Did you know that without even raising your voice, *you* have the authority to heal those that may be oppressed by demons? The second you came into relationship with Him, you were given that authority. You don't have to "work up" to it. The *moment* you became a citizen of heaven, you were given all the rights of those that come from that country. One of those rights? To be empowered by the Holy Spirit, not only for your own life, but also to take authority over spiritual wickedness in high places.

But not at the expense of being good.

We shouldn't be so focused on that empowerment that we forget to just do good things.

BE A DO-GOODER

Upsetters do good things. All the time. This is our lifestyle, how we live, how we want to go about our everyday life. Upsetters live every day asking God to put them in a position to do good and be good to someone that day. They're "do-gooders" because doing good shows His love—in action—to the world.

Let's continue that conversation about the importance of the true definition of words. There's often a negative connotation around the term "do-gooder," but this is what I love about Jesus: Jesus was a do-gooder in the truest sense of the word!

Out of all the miracles He could have chosen to start His ministry, He went to a wedding and—of all things—turned water into wine (John 2:1–11).

That was His first miracle.

Not blind eyes opening. A withered hand stretching out. A person that couldn't walk standing up. A dead man coming back to life. All that happened, too, but His *first* miracle?

Water into wine. Why?

Jesus was a *good guy*. He was just . . . *nice*.

There was a wedding going on and the host ran out of wine. Jesus happened to roll in with all the miraculous power embodied in Him. He could have done anything, been anywhere, but He went to a wedding. At some point people were muttering about how the wine ran out, Jesus' mom referred them to Him, and He just handled it.

Isn't that *thoughtful*?

Now, Jesus' mom *did* give Him a nudge—He didn't want to show His power at first, which I, personally, think just speaks to His humility. Can you imagine, when she first brought up the issue to Him, He said, "Woman, that's not our problem. . . . My time has not yet come" (John 2:4). But when she sent the servers to Jesus, He stepped up! I mean, He showed up in a Big Way. Scripture tells us He turned about 150 *gallons* of water into top-shelf wine, the kind that made the host wonder why the bridegroom saved "the good stuff" for the second half of the party.

Jesus was a "do-gooder"! This practical moment was the *first* way He shows up in all His miraculous glory. He met some partygoers in need at a wedding, and He just did something good for them.

DOING GOOD = BEING NICE

A little later, Jesus' ministry got established, and crowds were amassing to meet Him and hear Him preach. He turned to His disciples and said, "Hey, what should we feed them?"

His disciples *must* have done a double take at the crowd and then looked at Him like He was crazy. *"How?"*

Think about the sheer absurdity of this request at this moment. Maybe that absurdity is the reason why this is the only miracle recorded in all four Gospels (Matthew 14:13–21, Mark 6:32–44, Luke 9:10–17, and John 6:1–14)—none of the disciples could get over how nice Jesus was!

There were five thousand men out in that field—not including any women or children. There could have been as many as twelve to eighteen thousand people out there listening to Jesus' messages that day. And He was thinking, *Yeah, we should prolly feed 'em.*

I can just imagine the disciples stuttering: "I—hmm?—Us?— Again . . . *how*??"

He looked around for a second and said, "Anyone pack a lunch?"

Andrew came up going, "I have two fish and five loaves of bread. But I don't think—"

"Sit them down in groups of fifty."

This is like Hotel Management 101—almost as if Jesus has got restaurant experience!

He blessed the bread, broke it, started handing it out, and—this *is* a miracle—that bread and that fish did not stop until everyone had eaten.

Everyone.

Not, "Just the first ten people that got in line might get it *if* they're fast enough *and* in line early enough—there are registered seats for Jesus' conference, so if you didn't preregister, there's no meal ticket for you. There are food trucks outside, but *oops*, you're too late. None for you! You didn't get it."

Nope. He fed everybody!

That's. Just. *Nice!*

It was just nice for them to follow Him out into the middle of nowhere to hear Him preach, and then He fed them.

Here's another one. It was nice for Jesus to be walking around, see a short man in a tree, tell him to come down, and say, "Hey man, I'm coming to your house for dinner." It was just nice for the *Messiah*—who people had only been hoping for and expecting for about four thousand years—in the midst of everything He had to do on the way to going to die on the cross, to just decide to have dinner at Zacchaeus's house. Just because He felt like it. (See Luke 19, or wait until chapter 19 of this book when we talk about Zac a little more.)

Jesus was just nice.

There was a religious man named Nicodemus who had questions about who Jesus was. Jesus was nice enough to hang out with the guy late at night and answer his questions. Because He's a nice guy.

Jesus was just nice. Upsetters do good. We should be genuinely nice.

Upsetters do good. We should be genuinely nice. That's the only way we're going to get people to the Basement.

REMOVE THE LINES

Maybe you think that's not your personality. Maybe you're just "not a people person."

Nope. You don't get to be a believer in Jesus Christ and not be a people person.

Before you met Jesus, maybe you were a standoffish person, but if you start making boundary lines in your mind of where Jesus can and cannot have access to change your heart and change who you are for His sake . . . if you do it here, with people, you will also do it in your troubles.

Be careful. The enemy is looking for where you have drawn the line and not submitted to Christ's lordship, because wherever you draw the line, he's going to create more lines for you to cross so you can be in *his* territory.

If you draw a line in who you'll hug, maybe you'll draw a line in who you'll be willing to talk to as well. And if the enemy can get you to *not* talk to someone when the Holy Spirit nudges you to invite someone to the Basement, then that person never gets to hear what God has to say through you and the enemy wins that battle.

Don't let the enemy forget that he already lost the war.

Scripture References

Acts 10:38
John 14:15–18

John 2:1–11
Matthew 14:13–21
Mark 6:32–44
Luke 9:10–17
John 6:1–14
Luke 19:1–10

Practical Matters

Ask the Lord if you have any areas in your life where you've drawn boundary lines and won't let Him cross. Give those to Him and ask how you can just be nice to others in your daily life.

_____

_____

_____

_____

Notes

What is God saying to you?

_____

_____

_____

_____

fifteen

UPSETTERS LOVE LIFE

*I*f there's anything I loathe as it relates to communicating the gospel message, it's when pastors are motivational just for the sake of being motivational. Real motivation toward the gospel has to be empowered by a person—that is, the Holy Spirit. Otherwise it's just a pep talk, and we could get that anywhere. You don't have to get up on Sunday and be at the church for the 10 a.m. service or any of that if all you're looking for is a pep talk.

So when the Holy Spirit gave me "upsetters love life" as I was working on this, it kind of rubbed me the wrong way at first. It sounded too hippy-beachy-preachy.

"Just love life, man! Just go out there and get it! Love your life with a passion. Pursue it with abandon! Just go after it, and Jesus will be with you no matter what!" (Please feel free to read that with your most stereotypical, laid-back surfer impression—I am.)

Have you heard these sound bites before? I know I have.

Remember how I said I'm a literalist? I hear these things, and I think, *No matter what? I don't think Jesus will be with you* no matter *what.*

145

So I started asking the Holy Spirit for help, and do you want to know where He sent me?

> Live a life filled with love, following the example of Christ. He loved us and offered himself as a sacrifice for us, a pleasing aroma to God.
>
> —EPHESIANS 5:2

Well. That simplified things, didn't it?

So how can you live a life filled with love?

Live a life following the example of Christ, and not only will your life be filled with love but you will love the life you live. Seriously, that fixed the *whole* thing for me!

If I live a life following the example of Jesus Christ, then I will love the life that I live.

I can tell you with certainty that before I gave my life to Jesus Christ, what I thought I loved about my life, I really didn't. I loved some *parts* of it. I loved the highlight reel. But I wasn't in love with my entire life. When I gave my life to Jesus Christ and started following His example, I started to love the life that I was living because I had a blueprint on how to really live it.

So when I tell you to love your life, that upsetters love life and that they should be zestfully enthusiastic about life, what I'm really saying is that if you live a life following the example of Jesus Christ, you will love the life that you live.

ARE YOU LIVING THE HIGHLIGHT REEL?

Let me ask you this—and again, it's just us, so be honest—do you love your life? If you do, great! But it's okay if the answer is no. As a

If I live a life following the example of Jesus Christ, then I will love the life that I live.

matter of fact, that's fantastic, because it means you're ready to hear some good news!

Guess what? You really can love your life.

I'm not saying just ignore everything negative that's going on and "think happy thoughts" with a sprinkle of Jesus glitter—that's motivational, and we already talked about how I'm not here for any of that. That's ridiculous, and it doesn't last.

The joy of the Lord being your strength (Nehemiah 8:10) doesn't come from you plopping yourself in front of a mirror and force-smiling, saying,

"I'm just going to be happy until I'm happy!"
"If I think positive thoughts, positive things will happen!"
"If I think and have positive energy, it'll come!"

Are you growling in the mirror when you say those things? Because I feel like the grin of your "grin and bear it" is more like a struggling growl.

How about . . . not? Not trying to force a fake joviality of what you *think* it means to experience the joy of the Lord even if it kills you. Not ignoring that there are negative, sometimes truly difficult things going on in your life by "thinking positive thoughts."

Let's be real—there have been some incredibly dark moments in my life. I didn't love those moments, but I still love my life. Because there's a Person in it who completely overturned everything I thought about life and gave me a proper perspective on it. For that very reason, and following His example, I really *do* love my life.

Do bad things happen? Yes. Absolutely. I'm not Superman. I don't wake up every morning and throw open my curtains going,

"This is the best day *ever!*" to the tune of "Everything Is Awesome," like in *The Lego Movie.*

DROP THE FAKE GRIN

You might say to me, "You don't know my past, what I come from. God can't use me."

I don't have to know your past. I know mine. And if that's not enough, here's more evidence of when God overturned the lives of people who were in dire circumstances and inspired them to love their lives. Invariably, those upturned lives changed the world around them for good. Think about when you've seen God take broken, scared, lost people and used them to turn their world upside down:

- When a weak person like Gideon turned into a mighty man of valor.
- When a prostitute named Rahab became a redeemer of people who were not her own.
- When the murderer Moses became an ambassador for one of the greatest deliverances in human history.
- When God redeemed David's mistake and still called him a man after His own heart.
- When God took Peter's denial and turned him into a deliverer.
- When Paul, a persecutor, became the most passionate of the *persecuted.*
- When God took timid, timid Timothy and turned him into a tried-and-tested preacher with the boldness to declare his faith.
- When Thomas the doubter became the great evangelist to India. (Did you know that's where tradition says that Thomas

Think about when you've seen God take broken, scared, lost people and used them to turn their world upside down.

ended up? That's why some Christians in India still take the name Thomas as well as names like Matthew, John . . . They're named after the disciples of Jesus. That's how far-reaching the legacy of what God did through one man is.)

You want to love your life? Follow the example of Jesus, learn to accept the negative and grow past it with His help, and you will love the life you're in. Right now. Because let me tell you, He can redeem *any* life, *any* circumstance, *any* darkness, *any* legacy, *any thing*.

Scripture References

Ephesians 5:2
Nehemiah 8:10

Practical Matters

Would you be against throwing away your highlight reel to focus on loving the life you live?

_____

_____

_____

_____

_____

_____

How can you give God those hard or difficult moments and let Him upset your life?

_____

_____

_____

_____

What could happen if you let God upset your fake moments and started loving the life you live? Who could you impact around you?

_____

_____

_____

_____

Notes

What is God saying to you?

_____

_____

_____

_____

_____

part four

DISTURBING
THE PIECE

sixteen

THE PIECE,
NOT THE PEACE

This one is for my fellow nerds.

As a refresher, we've been talking a lot about the importance of the actual definition of words, right?

I believe we've been called and commissioned as believers to upset the world and disturb the piece. Some people might hear me say that out loud and say, "Oh great! I've already got my banner from the last Christians Against (fill in the blank) protest!"

No. Not disturbing the P-E-A-C-E like picketing, rallying, condemning, and judging. That's going back to the "anger" definition of "upset." Not what I mean. Not why we're here.

We're talking about disturbing the P-I-E-C-E. The piece of people's lives that is not arranged, in order, and in harmony with God's will, His way, His decrees. As ambassadors of an embassy, we've been commissioned to upset others by disturbing the piece of them that's not in harmony with Jesus Christ.

We've been called
and commissioned
as believers to
upset the world
and disturb
The piece.

Ain't that *nasty*?

(Like "upset," the word "nasty" has a positive connotation and a negative connotation. I'm using the positive at this moment because I *might* be here to disturb *your* piece a little today!)

So! Let's go back to Acts 17. Look at that biblical example of Paul and Silas disturbing the piece:

> Not finding them there, they dragged out Jason and some of the other believers instead and took them before the city council. "Paul and Silas have caused trouble all over the world," they shouted, "and now they are here disturbing our city, too."
>
> —ACTS 17:6

Again, I'm a literalist, so let's look at the definition of another word from that verse:

> Disturb (v.): to interfere with the arrangement, order, or harmony of, to disarrange.

I want you to think about a time in your life when you encountered God. When you were in His presence and He disturbed your piece. When He disturbed a paradigm of thought, a deeply held belief, a habit that you'd been holding on to for a long time. All of a sudden, He came in and disturbed that piece of your life to the point that what was previously neatly arranged in your mind got totally rearranged, unharmonized, and *turned upside down*. Now, you can't help but see it from heaven's perspective.

Turned upside down. Hold on. That sounds *a lot* like upsetting . . .

I told you this one was for the nerds!

IT'S TIME TO GO DEEP

In the next few chapters, I want to show you four moments in Jesus' ministry when He disturbed people's piece. If the question is, "How do we disturb the piece as upsetters?" we need a primer for what God does in our lives and in the lives of others so we can go out and disturb the piece in His name.

It is quite literally a blueprint for an invitation. But we'll get to that.

Since I'm talking to the nerds here, and I know good nerds take notes, I'm going to go ahead and spoil what you're about to read.

How Do We Disturb the Piece?

1. Pick the Place
2. Pick the Person
3. Pick the Piece

We're going to look at a few places in Scripture where Jesus didn't just address a situation that came to Him, He purposefully and strategically found a situation to address . . . and He's the one that instigated it.

Okay, admittedly, that was a little esoteric. What do I mean by that?

There are all types of moments in Scripture and in the Gospels where people are coming up to Jesus with their issues and begging Him to solve something for them.

"I want you to heal my sick loved one."
"I want you to raise this person from the dead."
"I want you to heal me."

Those were all people that came *to* Jesus, but I want to show you four instances when Jesus was the one who initiated contact. He strategically picked the place, the person, and the piece that He wanted to deal with, and He started upsetting things.

Scripture Reference

Acts 17:6

Practical Matters

Before we go out and disturb anyone else, let's pause and take an introspective moment with the Holy Spirit. After all, "why worry about a speck in your friend's eye when you have a log in your own?" (Matthew 7:3). Please hear what I'm saying: you *don't* have to be perfect to be an upsetter. But how likely is someone to hear your invitation to the Basement when you're living with one foot in the door, one foot out yourself?

Is there a piece of your life that God wants to disturb? What paradigms of thought, deeply held beliefs, or habits does He want to address for you?

_____

_____

_____

_____

Notes

What is God saying to you?

_____

_____

_____

_____

_____

_____

_____

_____

_____

_____

_____

_____

_____

_____

_____

_____

_____

_____

seventeen

PICK THE PLACE

Normally in a book like this, the author would start the chapter with a verse, then expound on it, *maybe* breaking it down in between.

I would like to be a little more intentional, if you'll indulge me.

Jesus knew the Pharisees had heard that he was baptizing and making more disciples than John (though Jesus himself didn't baptize them—his disciples did). So he left Judea and returned to Galilee. *He had to go through Samaria on the way.*

—JOHN 4:1–4

It's kind of funny that the scripture says Jesus *had* to go through Samaria on the way. He's *Jesus*. He can pretty much go wherever He wants to. But as a Jewish man, His people had been in contention with the Samaritans for centuries. Most Jews never wanted to come in close proximity to them—they literally went miles out of their way to go around Samaria. That would have been the case for the journey Jesus was taking: traveling from Judea in the south to Galilee in the north required either going through Samaria or taking a lengthy detour that added days of travel. Most Jewish people in that day would have taken the long route.

When the scripture says Jesus *had* to go through Samaria, I think it means He was being *very* intentional about picking the place to come in contact with a person to disturb their piece.

The place that He chose was Samaria.

COMING TO SAMARIA

Soon a Samaritan woman came to draw water, and Jesus said to her, "Please give me a drink."

—JOHN 4:7

He's picked His person. Remember, Jews didn't even talk to Samaritans. Jesus strategically chose this person because by merely opening His mouth to speak to her, He created a divine appointment. Trust and believe that Jesus isn't going to open His mouth and talk to you unless He *really* has something to say.

This woman came to the well. Without going into a historical deep dive, the women of this time would go to the well in the morning to draw the water and take it back to their homes. It was warmer in the middle of the day, and they were all doing their best to avoid being out in the worst of the heat. The fact that this woman came around noon—right as the heat of the day reaches its height—tells us that she was really trying hard not to be there around the other women.

He was being very intentional about picking the place to come in contact with a person to disturb their piece.

I don't know if you knew this about the woman at the well—it's a pretty delicious chapter: she had been married a lot of times (on par with Elizabeth Taylor). When Jesus opened His mouth and started this conversation with her, she had no idea that she was about to have her piece disturbed.

Jesus knew.

They had a conversation about getting water and how Jesus wasn't even supposed to talk to Samaritans. Jesus told her that if she knew the type of water He spoke about, she'd never be thirsty again.

Can you imagine what her internal dialogue must have been? Again, remember her circumstance. It's *noon* and she's out hauling water just to avoid the town gossip.

She must have gone, "Please give me that water! Can you set something up at my house? That way, I don't have to keep coming back out here! There are rumors about me going all around the city, so that would be *great* to avoid. If you know about indoor plumbing, that would be revolutionary to my life and many others, Jesus."

Or something like that.

And Jesus, as He does, just said the most pointed, unexpected thing possible: "Go and get your husband."

THE SCRIPT, FLIPPED

The *moment* He said that, He disturbed her piece.

What piece of her did He disturb? It wasn't about Him being nosy or prying. He was disturbing the piece of her that was unstable. He disturbed her instability with His word.

She responded with, "I don't have a husband."

He goes, "You're right. Because you've had five, and the one you're with right now isn't even your husband."

That's pretty unstable.

She thought He must be a prophet, and they continued on with their conversation—you're welcome to read all of it in John 4:1–30.

But here's how it ended.

Jesus upset the Samaritan woman's piece. This woman then went back into her town and evangelized about a man who was completely different than the six other men she'd been in relationships with. A place in her life that was perpetually unstable became stable because someone was bold enough to disturb her piece.

THE HEART OF THE PROBLEM

Have you ever met anyone on their ninth job in eleven months, and all they have is excuses? "I tried, I really did. But it just didn't work out over there, so I had to leave. I had to quit, man. They don't get me."

No, *you* don't get you. *You are unstable.*

When He disturbs your piece, Jesus addresses the instability at the heart of your problems.

For all intents and purposes, Jesus' encounter with the woman at the well was a quiet invitation to change. When He disturbs *anyone's* piece, it's always a quiet invitation to change.

No one can be forced to change—it just doesn't work, and even if it seems to be working at first, I guarantee you it's temporary. Forced change, just like a forced grin, doesn't stick. This is why, when we disturb a person's piece—the part of their life that's out of alignment with God—it can't be a forced entry, nor can it be a forced extraction.

Jesus addresses the instability at the heart of your problems.

It's always an invitation. Disturbing a person's piece makes them aware of the change that needs to happen, and then *they* come to their own conclusion of what they want to do with it.

So when He said, "Correct, you've had five husbands, and the one you're living with now, you're not even married to," that vibrated in her spirit enough and triggered her enough to think, *There's something different about this guy and what He's saying.*

Remember, she had come out to this well for water *long* after every other woman in this community was done drawing their water, which we think is because she didn't want to face any of them or hear what any of them had to say about her life choices. But here came this man, not to hit on her but to issue an invitation. And whenever Jesus gives an invitation, it's decision time for the person whose piece has been disturbed.

Everything changed for this woman. She realized that someone cared enough for her to address the thing in her that even *she* didn't like.

You see, there's a piece in each one of us that we don't like to talk about, we don't like to touch, we don't even want to see or acknowledge that it's there. It just takes the right person to disturb it, give us permission to address it, and empower us to move away from it.

We need upsetters in the world who will pick places and people and address the pieces in their lives that they *think* are in harmony . . . and disturb those pieces with invitations to change.

Scripture Reference

John 4:1–30

Practical Matters

Is there a place the Holy Spirit keeps sending you back to? Maybe a place you frequent for dinner or even your local donut shop? Start praying for that place (or places), that God would show you why He keeps sending you there. I'm not saying set up a soapbox and start handing out tracts—this is not that book.

Spend some time with God asking Him what He wants you to see about this place and who He wants you to talk to there.

_____

_____

_____

_____

_____

Notes

What is God saying to you?

_____

_____

_____

_____

_____

eighteen

PICK THE PERSON

If we were sitting in person, you'd see me rubbing my hands together like I'm about to start a fire with my excitement because this one is a favorite:

> When Jesus arrived at Peter's house, Peter's mother-in-law was sick in bed with a high fever.
>
> —MATTHEW 8:14

Remember, Jesus picked a place, a person, and a piece of their lives that He would disturb. So! What's the place? Peter's house. Who's the person? Peter's mother-in-law.

> But when Jesus touched her hand, the fever left her. Then she got up and prepared a meal for him.
>
> —MATTHEW 8:15

I think that *has* to be my mother-in-law's same anointing. My mother-in-law will cook you food *right now*, and it will be *fantastic*.

This story in Scripture shows one more thing I love about Jesus. This moment is amazing because we see in real time the walking dichotomy that Jesus is both a regular Jewish guy *and also* the Son of God.

The way it plays out in movies and shows doesn't do the juxtaposition of both sides of His nature true justice. Most on-screen portrayals of Jesus go a couple of different directions. They either go with what I like to call Deep Jesus, where everything is just so somber the whole time. There's a tear perpetually in His eye, He hardly ever smiles, and He always speaks in monotone: "I have come. I *must* die for all of you." Or you get what I call Tra La La Jesus, where everything is great and sunshine: "I'm here for you! I'm full of grace!" Neither Deep Jesus nor Tra La La Jesus truly hits the depth of what Jesus did in every page of Scripture—it just doesn't feel *real* to me.

They forget that He's not the Lion *or* the Lamb. He's both/and. He's the Lion *and* the Lamb.

But here's the thing. Yes, Jesus is God. He was also just a regular Jewish guy. For all that divinity, most of this story is regular, relatable, human stuff. Jesus was walking around with His crew, and they just rolled up in Peter's house looking for a meal. But when Jesus saw that Peter's mom was sick, He decided to heal her.

I like to imagine that at least part of Jesus' motivation to heal Pete's mom was that He was hungry. I mean, of course He was filled with compassion for her being sick. But I can just see Him walking into that house, hungry after a long day of walking, and saying, "I heard your mother-in-law could cook. Wait, she's sick? That's not good at all." He strolls over to her room, grabs her by the hand, and

Yes, Jesus is God. But He was also just a regular Jewish guy. For all that divinity, most of this story is regular, relatable, human stuff.

says, "Be healed, woman, in My name." She immediately gets up and she cooks.

Notice that Peter didn't call Jesus over to his house to heal his mother-in-law. In His sheer niceness, Jesus decided to disturb that piece of her that was the problem: her sickness. And He just heals it.

YOU'RE UP

You might have an opportunity to disturb someone's piece the same way. Maybe a sickness in someone's body becomes apparent. God might ask you to pray for them.

Don't be a coward.

Don't overthink it.

Don't worry over whether you *should* or if they'll *like* it or if you'll get in a fight over your lunch break because of Carol's headache or Jim's arthritis pain.

Just pray for her. Just pray for him.

What if you ask them if you can pray, and they don't want you to pray for them? Pray for them anyway. It's prayer. They don't have to hear it. They don't even have to know you're doing it.

Everyone has this image of praying over someone like you have to hold both their hands and *act* like you're praying. "I bind this headache, in Jesus' name!"

Just pray for them, even if it's internal and you're across the breakroom while they go to town on their tuna sandwich.

Remember my story about the woman at my temp job? We never prayed in front of her—pretty sure my coworkers were too scared of her anyway. We prayed silently and consistently. We filled that place up with prayer, and what happened?

God disturbed her attitude anyway, and it changed the *whole place*.

DISTURBED SIGHT

A few years ago, the Holy Spirit put someone in my path. His name's Roy Rizwan. He is a Muslim man from Pakistan, and I feel like God chose him, like the Holy Spirit led me right to him. The piece I've been disturbing in him is the way he sees God.

As a Gentile, I recognize that I'm talking to a distant cousin when I talk to a faithful follower of Islam. This is because the covenant that was given to Abraham is a covenant the Muslims believe was given to them through Ishmael, whereas we, as believers of Christ, believe it's through Isaac. So I already have common ground with Roy, even though we obviously see that common ground through two different lenses. But because of the way the Holy Spirit prompted me to act and the things He's prompted me to say, I have already disturbed Roy's piece enough that he no longer relies solely on his imam for wisdom and prayer. He constantly calls me to see if I will pray with him, to run stuff by me, to have me advise him, or even to just get wisdom on a certain situation.

You might be on the edge of your seat thinking, *Is Roy a believer now? Did Tim win him to Christ? Has he renounced his faith in Islam? Is he in the Basement too?*

Nope. I'm believing for God to ultimately disturb his piece. The disturbance of the piece isn't our job alone. We can only instigate under the direction of the Holy Spirit. It's up to God to finish the job.

Disturbing someone's piece doesn't mean making every single conversation into an altar call. I believe a bit like St. Francis of

The disturbance
of the piece isn't
our job alone. We
can only instigate,
but it's up to God
to finish the job.

Assisi: I will preach the gospel, and sometimes I'll use words. (Not an exact quote, mind you, but it's my philosophy of impacting the world around me.) So when Roy asks for prayer about a situation at his job or a conflict he's facing, I'm not subverting the conversation and completely ignoring his issue, like, "Let me lead you to Jesus right now!" I'm not praying for an hour, hoping that *something* that I say is *the thing* that leads him to Christ that day. No, I'm there to pray about the work thing, counsel him on the conflict thing, and move on in simply building a relationship with him.

Because guess what? Heaven's not up there grading your prayer word count, waiting to tip the balance in your favor on someone's change. Can you even imagine the angels in conference? Glasses precariously perched on the edge of a nose, quill hovering over a transcription dripping with red correction ink . . . "There's a fifty-word minimum. And I only heard four 'Father Gods.' I need at least twenty of them to even bring this to His attention."

FALSE REQUIREMENTS

That might sound ridiculous, but so many people are out there praying, "Father God, in the name of Jesus, Father God, bind this headache right now, in Jesus' name, Father God, cause you know, Father God, You are awesome. Cause Father God, cause Father God, cause Father God, and in Jesus' name, Father God, Father God . . ."

No, that's not a typo or a printing error. I have actually *heard* prayers like that, and I know you have too!

Listen—I can't stand "Father God" prayers. When I hear them, I forget what you're praying for! Honestly? Now I'm more focused on counting your "Father Gods" than on agreeing with you in prayer!

You're at twenty-two, and I thought we were just blessing the *food*. It's cold now! Stop that.

You know exactly what I'm talking about.

Where else would you do that?

You would not come up to the drive-thru and talk like that to Robert, who's at the window taking your order. In reality, you would *not* go, "Robert. Oh, Robert, Robert . . . Robert, can I have a burger? Robert? Oh, Robert, Robert, can I have a burger? And Robert, Robert, also a large fry? Oh, Robert, do the orange drink. Oh, Robert, Robert, Robert. Robert, can I have two pies for ninety-nine cents?" I can just hear the organ crescendo in there.

Robert would be leaning out the drive-thru window, wondering why you're sweating so hard, where the organist is hiding, and why you have accompaniment while you're ordering your meal— not to mention he's probably annoyed that you're holding up the dinner rush!

If that's how you pray with the person you've been sent to instigate into being disturbed, they may have moved from mildly interested in this Jesus guy and this Basement you've been talking about to highly annoyed, behind on their workday, and hungry for their lunch—all because they stopped to ask you to pray for their meeting with the boss this afternoon. They weren't counting on missing a whole meal. They just wanted you to pray.

So, what should you do?

Just pray.

Scripture Reference

Matthew 8:14–15

Practical Matters

Has the Holy Spirit highlighted a person to you who needs a piece disturbed? Write their name here and just start praying for them. This isn't the time to approach them—not yet, let them eat—that might come later. Now is just a time to hear what God might have to say about them and pray for them in ways they've expressed they need.

Who is God placing on your heart?

_____

_____

_____

_____

_____

Think about the place or places God gave you in the last chapter. Is there anyone there He's highlighting to you who might need something in their well-ordered life disturbed?

_____

_____

_____

_____

_____

_____

Notes

What is God saying to you?

_____

_____

_____

_____

_____

_____

_____

_____

_____

_____

_____

_____

_____

_____

_____

_____

_____

_____

nineteen

PICK THE PIECE

Okay, so we talked about Zacchaeus back in chapter . . . 14. If you said that before I did, you get bonus points!

Anyway, we talked about Zacchaeus when we were talking about Jesus just being a nice guy. But let's take a deeper look at what was going on in that story. We need the context of what Jesus was actually doing in order to see how He upset a place, a person, and a piece.

> Jesus entered **Jericho** and made his way through the town. There was a man there named **Zacchaeus**. He was the chief tax collector in the region, and he had become very rich. He tried to get a look at Jesus, but he was too short to see over the crowd. So he ran ahead and climbed a sycamore-fig tree beside the road, for Jesus was going to pass that way.
>
> When Jesus came by, he looked up at Zacchaeus and called him by name. "Zacchaeus!" he said. "Quick, come down! I must be a guest in your home today."

Zacchaeus quickly climbed down and took Jesus to his house in great excitement and joy. But the people were displeased. "He has gone to be the guest of a notorious sinner," they grumbled.

Meanwhile, Zacchaeus stood before the Lord and said, "I will give half my wealth to the poor, Lord, and if I have cheated people on their taxes, I will give them back four times as much!"

Jesus responded, "Salvation has come to this home today, for this man has shown himself to be a true son of Abraham. For the Son of Man came to seek and save those who are lost."

—LUKE 19:1–10

What's the place? _____ Who's the person? _____ Your note-taking skills are *killing* it. I love you! You're amazing! (If you weren't taking notes, I've got you. The answers are helpfully enlarged in the scripture above. You're welcome.)

Okay, can we pause for just a second? Because this is *fantastic*—it doesn't get much better than this. Jesus—again, just a normal Jewish guy going about His day—sees a short guy in a tree, tells him to come down, and then *invites Himself over for dinner*.

What?!

I just love Jesus—He already knew Zacchaeus's reputation and decided to show up anyway.

Kind of like He did in every single one of our lives.

He knew your reputation but decided to move right into your heart anyway. Even though He already knew everything you've done, everything you've been, He just moves right in there with you.

What's the piece He decided to disturb that day at Zacchaeus's house?

Rejection.

He knew your reputation but decided to move right into your heart anyway.

WHERE'S YOUR IDENTITY?

As a tax collector, Zacchaeus, a Jewish man, had made a *lot* of money from overtaxing his own people. He became a wealthy man with a lot of influence. You know what the problem was? He found his security and his identity in his wealth because he was covering a massive hole of rejection.

Where do I see that in the scripture? Look at the text and look at the context.

Here's a hard truth: I don't know many short men who would climb a tree just to get a peek at Jesus. Just to have Jesus notice them. Then, when He notices them, get *so* excited they have to throw a party in His honor.

Here is my conclusion: he had never been affirmed by anyone else!

When Zacchaeus heard Jesus say, "Hey, Zac, come down! I want to go to your house!" it wasn't because he was rich, it wasn't because of his name or his influence in the community. It was because He saw the man in a *tree*, and that attention immediately poked at the piece of Zacchaeus's life that Jesus wanted to disturb.

There are a lot of people reading this who own businesses and have become very wealthy, and—this makes me happy—their identity is in Christ, not in their success. Because if your identity is in your success, that's because it's covering something on the inside of you that feels rejected.

When we feel that rejection—whatever its source—we turn to our vocation, our bank accounts, or our degrees on the wall to affirm us.

But those temporary things can never affirm you like the one who created you.

Jesus disturbed that piece of rejection that had found a home in

Zacchaeus's heart. The man responded by *giving away* the wealth in which he'd found his identity.

LEX TALIONIS

You have to understand the Jewish context of what he said, though: "And if I have cheated people on their taxes, I will give them back four times as much!" (Luke 19:8). The tax collectors of the day were *notorious* for scalping members of their own community to line their own pockets—it's why everyone hated Zacchaeus! He didn't get rich by doing everything right! But here he's going over and above what the Pentateuch requires of someone paying restitution if they've been unfair. This is the principle of *lex talionis*, where the punishment mirrors the crime—an eye for an eye (Leviticus 24:19–21). But Zacchaeus goes *way* beyond the expected restitution of the day and quadruples what's due to those he wronged.

Thinking about the impact of this, look no further than popular culture and how many celebrities seemingly "have it all." They have the money, the status, the influence, the toys, the cars, the planes, the access to exotic locales . . . But how many of them routinely check *themselves* into rehab? They've reached the penthouse of life, but they have no peace, so they try to make up for it with drug abuse and alcohol abuse.

Michael Jackson? King of pop. Rich as can be. The man had anything and everything he could possibly want. But he needed a powerful tranquilizer just to go to sleep.

The majority of us are wealthier than Michael Jackson, and we don't even know it. Why? Because at the end of the day, we can lie down, put our heads on our own pillows, and *just go to sleep*.

MOUNT EVEREST

Every year, 300–400 people attempt to climb the tallest mountain in the world, Mount Everest. Records estimate that 322 people have died attempting to summit the mountain. That averages out to around four and a half deaths a year, though the number of deaths is increasing with seventeen deaths in the 2023 season. As intoxicating as it is for us to go up, we were meant to live low.

I believe God gave us gravity to remind us that we need to remain grounded. Looking at MJ, all I can think about is the myriad ways humanity tries to go against gravity. But it takes exponentially more effort to go up than it does to come down. While I enjoy the benefits and efficiencies of air travel, we have to burn fossil fuel by the millions of gallons just to get up in the air. That fuel burn is a reminder that we're going against natural forces.

Think about it. As an astronaut or a fighter pilot, you have to go through rigorous physical preparation and training to be able to withstand what the pressures of flight do to your body. Even the sheer physical toll on a normal human body on a commercial flight is insane! Any time you're on an extended flight, the flight attendants will remind you—multiple times!—to get up and walk around because the threat of deep vein thrombosis is *real*. The cramps. The dehydration. Your ears popping in the pressurized cabin.

It's cool to watch a plane. It's cool to watch a bird. It's cool to watch SpaceX shoot their next rocket full of human beings up into the atmosphere, but we were not designed to rise. That's why the falls are so devastating and destructive. Look at Michael Jackson, Prince, and every pastor who has fallen from grace—all those crazy stories of what happens when we have a meteoric rise to success.

The air gets thin. The judgment gets cloudy. To fill the void of trying to stay up at that level, we numb ourselves with alcohol, with drugs, with sex, with porn. We become prideful, narcissistic, demanding, and entitled. Inevitably, the fall happens, and we're brought plummeting back to earth.

Those in pop culture and among celebrities who do find a relationship with Christ—like a Chris Pratt or a Letitia Wright or a Denzel Washington—tend to move about with a freedom that others in their industry often don't experience. Rejection doesn't seem to find them in a tangible way, and neither does that desperate fall. They have no interest in the penthouse because they've already reached the Basement.

Arguably, they have the same skill set, the same contacts in the industry, the same zip code, and maybe even the same work ethic.

The only difference? Their relationship with Christ.

See, God is constantly looking for places where He can disturb the piece of someone's life that feels out of alignment with Him, and here's where you know Jesus is healing that piece of rejection in Zacchaeus. He tells the man, "You're a true son of Abraham."

Not just because Zacchaeus can trace his bloodline back that far. Not just because he's related to Abraham. He's *acting* like Abraham because he's placing his faith in God.

Keep in mind, the lineage of Abraham was based on blood, yes, but it was and is also based on faith and trusting God, even when His following through seems unlikely or even implausible—if not impossible. By exercising his faith that day, Zacchaeus stepped out of who he had been, and Jesus recognized that, reaffirming his connection to Abraham's lineage of faith.

That busted his piece—that place of rejection—wide open and brought freedom into Zacchaeus's life.

God is constantly looking for places where He can disturb the piece of someone's life that feels out of alignment with Him.

Scripture References

Luke 19:1–10
Leviticus 24:19–21

Practical Matters

If you've been paying attention and taking notes, you'll hopefully grasp where we're going here. Think of the person and place or people and places that God's been speaking to you about over the past two chapters.

What are the pieces in these places and for these people that the Holy Spirit wants to disturb?

_____

_____

_____

_____

_____

_____

Ask God for some practical ways you can upset those pieces. Remember, we're not here to hit anyone over the head with our Bibles. We're talking quiet invitations for them to decide to meet with Jesus. We're here to instigate people toward a conversation with Jesus, not shove them in His direction.

What can you do to instigate?

_____

_____

_____

_____

_____

_____

_____

Notes

What is God saying to you?

_____

_____

_____

_____

_____

_____

_____

_____

Twenty

HIGHWAYS, BYWAYS, BUSHES, AND SHRUBS

Okay, I want to get really practical for you here. I could come up with a scenario, but guess what? God already did it for me. Let's look at two scriptures:

Jesus also told them other parables. He said, "The Kingdom of Heaven can be illustrated by the story of a king who prepared a great wedding feast for his son. When the banquet was ready, he sent his servants to notify those who were invited. But they all refused to come!

"So he sent other servants to tell them, 'The feast has been prepared. The bulls and fattened cattle have been killed, and everything is ready. Come to the banquet!' But the guests he had invited ignored them and went their own way, one to his farm, another to his business. Others seized his messengers and insulted them and killed them.

"The king was furious, and he sent out his army to destroy the murderers and burn their town. And he said to his servants, 'The wedding feast is ready, and the guests I invited aren't worthy of the honor. Now go out to the street corners and invite everyone you see.' So the servants brought in everyone they could find, good and bad alike, and the banquet hall was filled with guests.

"But when the king came in to meet the guests, he noticed a man who wasn't wearing the proper clothes for a wedding. 'Friend,' he asked, 'how is it that you are here without wedding clothes?' But the man had no reply. Then the king said to his aides, 'Bind his hands and feet and throw him into the outer darkness, where there will be weeping and gnashing of teeth.'

"For many are called, but few are chosen."

—MATTHEW 22:1–14

Then Luke records the same moment. It's the same story, just worded a little differently because it's heard by different ears. Let's take a look:

Hearing this, a man sitting at the table with Jesus exclaimed, "What a blessing it will be to attend a banquet in the Kingdom of God!"

Jesus replied with this story: "A man prepared a great feast and sent out many invitations. When the banquet was ready, he sent his servant to tell the guests, 'Come, the banquet is ready.' But they all began making excuses. One said, 'I have just bought a field and must inspect it. Please excuse me.' Another said, 'I have just bought five pairs of oxen, and I want to try them out. Please excuse me.' Another said, 'I just got married, so I can't come.'

"The servant returned and told his master what they had

said. His master was furious and said, 'Go quickly into the streets and alleys of the town and *invite the poor, the crippled, the blind, and the lame.*' After the servant had done this, he reported, *'There is still room for more.'* So his master said, 'Go out into the country lanes and behind the hedges and *urge anyone you find to come,* so that the house will be full. For none of those I first invited will get even the smallest taste of my banquet.'"

—LUKE 14:15–24

SHRINKING INTO THE BUSHES

I have a visual for this. Ready?

Every time I see these scriptures, all I can think about is the GIF of Homer Simpson from *The Simpsons* shrinking back into the bushes. Do you know the one? His hands and arms are paralyzed next to his body, and his eyes have that deer-in-the-headlights look going on as if to say, "Nope. Nuh-uh. Not me."

See, Homer's not the first person to shrink into some shrubs. This has been going on since the beginning. Since Genesis. Since Adam and Eve themselves.

This has been happening since the beginning of humanity! People have been hiding in the bushes and shrubs, and it takes a certain disposition and boldness to go after those people. Normally we're scared—terrified even—of people who are hiding in bushes because we think they're getting ready to jump out and attack us. It takes a certain boldness and fearlessness to look behind the bushes and shrubs and say, "You don't have to hide here anymore. We already know you're naked."

God came walking through the garden of Eden (the place) in

the cool of the day, looking for Adam and Eve (the people), asking "Where are you?" When they respond, "We hid ourselves because we were naked," He doesn't question their hiding; He questions their *purpose* for hiding: "Who told you that you were naked?" (the piece—Genesis 3:11).

This is the reality of what it looks like to pick the place, pick the person, and pick the piece. It's having the boldness to push through the bushes, peel away the masks and veils and costumes people are hiding behind, and gently invite them out—nakedness and all.

UNDERSTAND THE ASSIGNMENT

Highways, byways, bushes, and shrubs is the assignment of everybody who has been upset, of everyone who has come to the Basement. You need to come down here and get equipped so that you can go out there and actually relate to some people—*real* people. These passages of scripture let us know that there are already people at the banquet table, people that already gave their life to Jesus, that made a commitment to Him. They're sitting at the Master's table in the Basement, and do you know what He's saying? "I still have room. Go out and get some more."

As a church we've become too complacent. We're so happy our buildings are full. We're so happy when we make it to four services. Do you think the Master's saying, "Good for you! Good job! Thirty thousand people in ten years!" Maybe, but guess what? There are seven *million* people right here where I am in the Dallas Metroplex. We haven't even made a *dent* in this city!

That assignment might seem impossible. Luckily, He's not relying on any one individual to go out and personally invite all the millions and billions of people around the world into the Basement. This assignment is for *all* of us. By saying, "I still have room," He's asking the whole body of Christ to go out and invite more.

He'll call another person to build another church in the same way that nearly every city around the world always has another chain restaurant popping up and no one gets tired of it. No one complains when another Hopdoddy opens! No one is out there yelling, "We don't want your delicious burgers and your crispy fries! We've already got a McDonald's. We've already got a Hardee's (or Carl's Jr. depending what part of the country you live in)." No, they're lining up for it!

Did you know that when In-N-Out first came to Texas in the summer of 2010, people lined up for over *two hours* in the heat for their made-to-order burgers, shakes, and fries? Two whole hours! And no one was mad about it—them jokers were all too excited to eat those burgers, shakes, and fries! And I was one of them! I sat in that long line and then *happily* ate that burger!

DISTURBING THE PIECE IN REAL TIME

Remember the mandate the Holy Spirit gave me that I shared in the introduction? He said, "Bring as many people to the Basement as you can." He didn't say to go get saved people, or people on the fence, or Christians who've never left their church bubble. He said go get as many people to the Basement as you can.

That's why I did the podcast. That's why I left the pulpit. People are concerned, asking why I don't preach in as many churches or if I've turned my back on God. They think I'm just out there in the secular world. No, I haven't turned my back on God. I'm out here looking in the

By saying, "I still have room," He's asking the whole body of Christ to go out and invite more.

highways, byways, bushes, and shrubs. We've been able to reach people with this platform that we *never* would have through my preaching.

Agnostics. Atheists. Deconstructionists. People in the LGBTQIA+ community. People in the adult film industry, whether that's actual porn stars, strippers, or OnlyFans performers. Basketball players, football players, models, actors, actresses, directors, producers, musicians, you *name* it!

People who would have *never* been compelled to listen to clips of me preaching behind a pulpit or on a stage speaking to who knows how many people in their Sunday best are compelled by me just talking and having conversations with regular, normal people living out their daily lives. And most of the time, we're just in sweats and T-shirts!

For twenty-seven and a half years, I was one of the hosts and waiters at my Father's banquet table. After twenty-seven years, He tapped me on the shoulder and said, "Hey son, you've done a good job waiting tables here. I love the food you've brought out and served My people. But I need you to go out there."

I looked where He was pointing and shook my head. "I'm more comfortable in here. I know how to dress here. I'm familiar with the people here. I'm familiar with the menu here."

But God was *adamant*. "Just go out there."

Concern set in, if I'm honest, because I was being stubborn. "But God, the way I talk out there to reach those people is a little bit different than the way I talk in Your restaurant."

"It's okay."

So many questions popped up in my head. "Well, I'm gonna get canceled if I say some of the things that I need to say to reach these people that are in the highways, byways, bushes, and shrubs. They're not always as 'refined' as the people who have been sitting at the table for a while." (I say "refined" with so much sarcasm.)

He just smiled and said, "Yeah, go ahead and get canceled. I'm with you. They don't have to understand your assignment. I do because I'm the one that gave it to you. Now, go."

So I took off my little cummerbund, popped off that little clip-on tie, and ran straight out into these streets to reach these people. And I cannot be satisfied. I don't care how many people are at the banquet table in the Basement—there are still more out there in the highways, byways, bushes, and shrubs than there are at my Master's table.

Those of us who have just been sitting at the banquet table for years and years stuffing our bellies with this good food at the Master's house need to push the plate back and actually go outside into the highways, byways, bushes, and shrubs to get someone and bring them back to the table.

Scripture References

Matthew 22:1–14
Luke 14:15–24
Genesis 3:11

Practical Matters

Do you understand the assignment or are you, like Homer, shrinking back into the bushes? Are you lingering at the table rather than going out and presenting the invitation to those around you who need to hear it?

_____

_____

_____

_____

_____

_____

_____

Ask God for some practical ways you can upset those pieces. Remember, we're not here to hit anyone over the head with our Bibles. We're talking quiet invitations for them to decide to meet with Jesus. We're here to instigate people toward a conversation with Jesus, not shove them in His direction.

What can you do to instigate?

_____

_____

_____

_____

_____

_____

_____

_____

_____

Notes

What is God saying to you?

_____

_____

_____

_____

_____

_____

_____

_____

_____

_____

_____

_____

_____

_____

_____

_____

_____

_____

part five

FITTING IT ALL TOGETHER

Twenty-one

PUZZLE PIECES

We talked about what it means to be an upsetter and how only by allowing God to flip your life upside down will you become upset and choose to enter the Basement. We talked about how the only way to get others to the Basement is to upset them and gently invite them down. It's time to put it all together.

Let's go to Scripture:

When they came to a place called The Skull, they nailed him to the cross. And the criminals were also crucified—one on his right and one on his left.

Jesus said, "Father, forgive them, for they don't know what they are doing." And the soldiers gambled for his clothes by throwing dice.

The crowd watched and the leaders scoffed. "He saved others," they said, "let him save himself if he is really God's Messiah, the Chosen One." The soldiers mocked him, too, by offering him a drink of sour wine. They called out to him, "If you are the King of the Jews, save yourself!" A sign was fastened above him with these words: "This is the King of the Jews."

One of the criminals hanging beside him scoffed, "So you're the Messiah, are you? Prove it by saving yourself—and us, too, while you're at it!"

But the other criminal protested, "Don't you fear God even when you have been sentenced to die? We deserve to die for our crimes, but this man hasn't done anything wrong." Then he said, "Jesus, remember me when you come into your Kingdom."

And Jesus replied, "I assure you, today you will be with me in paradise."

By this time it was about noon, and darkness fell across the whole land until three o'clock. The light from the sun was gone. And suddenly, the curtain in the sanctuary of the Temple was torn down the middle. Then Jesus shouted, "Father, I entrust my spirit into your hands!" And with those words he breathed his last.

—LUKE 23:33–46

The place is the cross. The person is *us*.

The piece?

It's sin.

This is where we all live.

What Jesus did for the woman at the well was amazing. He disturbed her piece of instability and got her back in line and focused on not just *a* man but *the Man*.

What He did at Peter's house with his mother-in-law was just *nice*. He healed her sickness, disturbed that piece of her life, and she got back on her feet. Things were great.

What Jesus did for the woman at the well was amazing. He disturbed her piece of instability and got her back in line and focused on not just a man but The Man.

Then He noticed a man in a tree and decided to go to his house for dinner—even though He knew Zacchaeus's reputation and what people would say about Him in the process. (Now there's a guy who is *so* secure in His relationship with God that He doesn't care what you think.) While at Zacchaeus's house, Jesus dealt with his issue of rejection, and a tax collector found his whole world upset and turned upside down by a (seemingly) normal Jewish man who was just nice enough to have dinner with him and *not* think about anyone's reputation.

But this last moment right here on Golgotha?

You know, if the Bible was just an account of a guy who did nice things for a lot of people that didn't actually include us—that came thousands of years before us—we would all give a little golf clap and say, "Great story, bro. Wish I could have met Him."

Well . . . you *can*.

There's nowhere that Jesus *won't* go to meet the people who need Him. Samaria, where no other Jews would go. Peter's house. Zacchaeus's house, where no other rabbi would go because the tax collector was *disreputable*.

THE BEST THING THAT EVER HAPPENED

Can I just blow the lid off this for a second?

That God would come to *earth* . . .

That the God of heaven would wrap Himself in flesh, leave heaven, come here, and then *choose* a place like the cross to display His love for us!

Honestly, it would have been nice enough if He just came to

your house. If Jesus had spent the rest of human history just show-ing up at people's houses, that would have been *nice*.

But for Him to show up on a cross is something *exponentially* different.

Christ Jesus, who, though he was in the form of God, did not count equality with God a thing to be grasped, but emptied him-self, by taking the form of a servant, being born in the likeness of men. And being found in human form, he humbled himself by becoming obedient to the point of death, *even death on a cross.*

—PHILIPPIANS 2:5–8 ESV

Not just death, but "even death on a cross," as if to say this death is acutely worse than just death itself. You see, in Jesus' day, dying on a cross was the most acute form of humiliation and torture the Romans had. He literally died the worst way they could think of at the time. This was a death they sentenced criminals to—the worst of the worst.

That Jesus picked that particular place to display His love for *all of us*?

Can you imagine the angels' response to Him picking *this* place to show everyone a display of His love?

"Who would you do it for? Cause, you know, you have a cove-nant with these Jewish people you've been called to. If you're going to choose to die a horrible death—a criminal's death, by the way—on that cross, who are you going to do it for?" I imagine there must have been some hesitance in that question, maybe some stumbling over words because . . . could He possibly be *sure*?

But yes, He's sure. "Everybody."

"And—and what piece are you going to disturb in the process?"

"Sin."

"We saw what You did with sickness. We saw what You did with rejection. We saw what You did with instability—"

"Yeah, that's all a result of sin. I don't want to have to go down a list and keep checking stuff off individually, so let's just deal with the sin so we can wipe that out for everyone, and they can be back for the family reunion with Dad in the Basement. This could all just be over."

Here's the most upsetting thing that has ever happened in all of human history: That Jesus would disturb the *one piece* of existence that separates us from a relationship with God, the Father. Intentionally. On a cross. For all of *us*.

It's so upsetting, in fact, that time has been split to define before the guy died and after He died. That whole BC/AD thing? That came from some people in history who understood that there are a lot of important people who lived and who died, but *that right there*?

That is the best thing that's ever happened.

Scripture References

Luke 23:33–46
Philippians 2:5–8

Practical Matters

I know I've asked for this a few times before, but just in case you were masking or you weren't yet feeling vulnerable enough to go there yet, I'm going to ask this one again:

Here's the most upsetting thing that has ever happened in all of human history: That Jesus would disturb the one piece of existence that separates us from a relationship with God, the Father.

Is there a piece of your life that God wants to upset?

_____

_____

_____

_____

_____

_____

_____

Notes

What is God saying to you?

_____

_____

_____

_____

_____

_____

_____

_____

Twenty-Two

ARE YOU THE
MISSING PIECE?

Have you ever seen *The Accountant* with Ben Affleck and Anna Kendrick? It's about a guy on the autism spectrum. There's a scene where, as a kid, he's putting together a puzzle . . . face-down. He's a genius, so he gets it all done—but there is one missing piece, and he can't find it.

He freaks out a little. "I can't find it! I've gotta finish!"

I imagine God doing that with the puzzle of everything He's putting together on this earth. Just going crazy: "I've *got* to finish! You are the missing piece!"

It's not about us forgiving anyone of their sins—that's not our job—Jesus forgives people of their sins. But we can disturb that little subset piece of them that is blocking them from seeing the love of God in their lives.

As upsetters, *we* are commissioned to go out and upset others,

As upsetters, we are commissioned to go out and upset others, and I'm telling you, it doesn't have to be fanatical Bible waving or shouting from the street corners. You can just have fun.

and I'm telling you, it doesn't have to be fanatical Bible waving or shouting from the street corners. You can just have *fun*.

All you have to do is intentionally pick the place.

FOR ME, IT'S RESTAURANTS

I don't know what it is, but I'm really good at restaurants. Well, no, that's not entirely true . . . I know what it is: I'm hungry a lot. Or maybe I'm just anointed to upset people at restaurants.

I pick two or three restaurants, and I'm intentional about praying for everybody in there. I'm going to disturb them. I'm going to *get* them. *Everybody.*

How do I start disturbing people's piece? I start with hugs.

I will literally hug *everybody.*

The host who greets you at the door and is supposed to seat you. The server. The busboy. The manager who comes to check and see if your meal's going all right—*everybody.*

I just hold out my arms, and they might be a little confused at first, but eventually, it's like they can't help but hug back.

Even if it's a little awkward, I just smile, hold out my arms, and say, "Hi! Come, come!"

I go in there, order my food, act right, leave a good tip—without a card to Embassy City Church or any other church—and then go back and do it all over again. And again. And again.

When I go back, *they* go, "Come, come! So glad you're here!" And no matter how awkward it was at first, eventually *they* want to hug *me.*

Start doing that to two or three of the waiters and waitresses, and they start throwing elbows! They start fighting over who gets to serve your table!

"They're here!"

"I've got them!"

"No, I do!"

See, I'm in this for the *long* game. Sometimes, I can disturb people's piece the first time I meet them. Other times, it's the ninth time I meet them.

Eventually there's an opportunity where the Holy Spirit just helps you sense that there's some fear or some intimidation there . . . there's some rejection or instability there.

And however He talks to you, in whatever manner you hear His voice or feel the impression of what He wants you to do, you'll hear, "I want you to disturb *that*."

It doesn't matter if you're introverted or extroverted. All you have to do is ask the Holy Spirit to give you the boldness to just go tinker with that piece a little bit.

Ask if you can pray with them for that. Or follow the Holy Spirit's lead and say something to them that completely blows their mind.

HOW I INSTIGATE

One time, I was at the Cheesecake Factory—which I lovingly refer to as my northside office—for a lunch meeting. A young lady was serving our table, and for some reason the Holy Spirit kept saying, "She's beautiful . . . She's beautiful . . . She's beautiful . . ."

I didn't want to tell the young lady she was beautiful—I'm married! I didn't want her to think the wrong thing!

But the Holy Spirit kept saying the same thing over and over.

So I asked the guy I was eating with, "I want to run this by you. I feel like the Lord is telling me to tell this young lady that she's beautiful, but I don't want you to think that I'm hitting on her, so if you say I shouldn't, then I won't."

He looked at her, looked at me, and said, "Nah, bro. Tell her."

What could I say but "Okay"?

When she came back, I just said, "Hey, I just want to tell you, you're just such a beautiful person."

The girl almost lost it at the table. She literally went blank-faced, her eyes welled up, and she couldn't keep it together, so she walked away.

I was like, "Oh boy. *That* went well. Manager's probably coming now."

About ten minutes later, she came back, and she said, "I got adopted as a baby, and for my whole life, I've never felt like I was beautiful. Then you said that, and it hit something on the inside of me, and I don't even know what to do with it."

Guess what? I didn't turn it into a counseling session. I didn't have her sit down there in the booth so I could "tell her what she needs to do," or pray out loud for her. *An organ drops into the middle of the restaurant's parquet floor, and the lights dim: "Father God . . . Father God . . ."*

Ha! I'm sorry, I just couldn't resist that.

But no! I just said, "Well, I just felt like God told me to tell you that."

Booyah! Snuck a little God in there, and I was done.

The piece in her life that needed it has already been disturbed, and I'm out. I'm not here to close the deal and rehabilitate her life right there in the restaurant. I want to eat my fries and my turkey burger while they're hot! (They use the thigh meat—it's fantastic!)

Sorry, not sorry if you end up at the Cheesecake Factory after this book.

Maybe for you, it's not your northside office. Maybe it's Roscoe's Chicken and Waffles, In-N-Out, Wendy's, or that deliciously sweet little mom-and-pop BBQ place you love down the street where they sneak you free biscuits when they pack up your food. Maybe you're into DIY, and you're always at the hardware store or the garden store. Maybe you're the cook in your family, and you're always at the grocery store or the farmer's market. Maybe you always stop at the same gas station on the way to work. *Wherever* you find yourself frequenting, there are opportunities that God will give you, and when they arise, He'll give them to you according to your personality. You don't have to go out and look for it or hunt for it, going after it with Bible-thumping intensity.

Calm down.

The Holy Spirit will make it happen.

DO IT LIKE JESUS

Did you see all the places where it happened for Jesus? It all started so naturally.

He's at a well, a woman shows up, He asks for water, a whole conversation breaks out—disturbs her piece—her whole life gets changed, and people get saved.

Goes to Peter's house, and Peter's mother-in-law is sick. He goes into the room, prays for the mom—disturbs her piece—Mom gets well.

He's walking down the road, and Zacchaeus is in the tree. He goes, "Hey, can I come to your house?" Zacchaeus responds, "Yes!"—disturbs his piece—and Jesus upsets the rejection in his heart.

It's kind of organic!

Wherever you find yourself frequenting, There are opportunities That God will give you, and when They arise, He'll give Them To you according to your personality.

If you're at the gas station and the Lord says something to you about the person pumping gas next to you, go disturb their piece. If you're in the checkout line at Target, and the Holy Spirit whispers to you to tell the cashier something, disturb their piece. Then jump in your car, and—*drive off.* It doesn't have to turn into a revival!

I want to encourage you and exhort you to go disturb the piece. You probably already know some people. You probably have a co-worker, family member, or friend that you already know has a little piece that God's been whispering to you about—a piece that *if* it was disturbed, it would probably move some stuff out of the way so they could actually see Jesus for who He really is.

YOUR NIKE MOMENT

Here's how I want to end this book . . . not with an explosion of fireworks or a cheer or even an organist crashing on the keys in the middle of your quiet time or your reading space.

Just do it.

I'd rather not get you all hyped up. If I do and you don't do it, then it's just nice for this little book right here, a couple of good words on a few thin pages, some quiet time alone, etc.

It is somewhat anticlimactic, but I'd rather just ask you, "Would you be opposed to upsetting the world?"

Because if we did that, we would be doing what God put us on this earth to do. He put *you* in *your* city for a reason.

To bring this conversation full circle and go back to where we started in the introduction, there's a lot happening outside the pages of this illustrious tome in your hands: war, racial conflict, political tension, economic collapse. Everyone's angry and distressed, and everyone is trying to change everything all at once, all by shouting over one another unintelligibly, thinking if they could just shout louder, climb higher than the other person screaming to be heard as well, maybe just maybe they'd inflict change.

But if all anyone actually experiences is anger or distress, then they're just angry. They're all just yelling into the abyss, and nothing is actually *changing*.

If we want to bring about real change in people like the lady at my temp job, the woman at the well, the girl at the Cheesecake Factory, Peter's mother-in-law, Roy, or Zacchaeus . . .

If we want to bring about real, lasting change, we need to start with first allowing *ourselves* to be truly upset by the message of the gospel. Only then can we go out and start upsetting others in the same way—by the power and guidance of the Holy Spirit.

Becoming upsetters and changing what we think it means to be great is the only way to turn the world upside down—or, from heaven's perspective, bring the world right side up.

And it's not even just for your household and your family. It's for wherever you live, for the entire world around you. Dallas. New York. LA. Chicago. London. Paris. Tokyo. Sydney. Caracas. Cape Town. New Delhi. Kyiv. Berlin. Moscow. And all the way back to Washington, DC.

You want to experience change in the world around you?

Wherever you're from, it's simple, really. Go disturb the piece.

So. I'll ask you one more time, and then you can put this book down and go on about your life. But I really hope this sticks with you:

Would you be opposed to upsetting the world?

Practical Matters

Would you be opposed to upsetting the world?

_____

_____

_____

_____

_____

_____

Notes

What is God saying to you?

_____

_____

_____

_____

_____

_____

CONCLUSION

To My Dwellers

There's nothing else I can tell you. In these pages I dump everything out. I give you the vision. I walk you through practical applications of how to go about being great by coming down to the Basement and inviting others to do the same.

But before you go . . .

Lemme holler at you real quick. There's something I need you to know. You are walking out of the King's house and you have been given a mandate to go and make disciples. Beyond that, what we read in Matthew 22 and Luke 14 is literally a command to be a part of a search committee.

"I want you to leave my house and go find *everybody* that you can. *Any body.*" In Matthew it says to look for both good and bad alike—which means don't judge them when you walk up. Don't look at their outside and judge what might be on the inside. Don't even go to your preference.

This isn't about all Black people going into Black communities, or White people going into White communities, or Hispanics

God changed His invitation from those who thought they were too good to come down to a basement for a banquet to people who knew they wouldn't want to be anywhere else. All they needed was an invitation.

going into Hispanic communities, or Asians going into Asian communities.

He's asking *people* to go find *people*.

People who look like you, act like you, dress like you, talk like you, as well as people who don't look like you, don't act like you, don't dress like you, and don't talk like you.

Go find anybody and everybody you can and simply invite them to this feast.

Here is why I'm bringing this up: I don't know *anyone* who has ever invited someone to dinner and made it sound like bad news. I don't know anyone who has ever made an announcement like "Hey! Free food!" and made it sound like they're talking to inmates being summoned for lunch from the prison yard. They're not angry! When you're giving out something you know people are going to enjoy, there's an upward inflection in your voice that stirs excitement!

"Fam! Free food! Let me tell you something—my boss decided to throw this dope banquet. There were some people who were supposed to be here, and they decided not to come, which means there's a place at the table for you."

The invitation you're giving is good news. It is attractive. It should be so compelling that it makes it hard for them to say no.

But you have to remember the type of people He tells us to go after: the lame, the crippled, the blind, the broken.

Not the astute, not the affluent. Though, when I say that, please don't think you're not supposed to go after rich people and you're only supposed to go after poor people. I can point out *a lot* of crippled, lame, blind, broken, and paralyzed multimillionaires out there.

I'm saying God changed His invitation from those who thought they were too good to come down to a basement for a banquet to people who knew they wouldn't want to be anywhere else. All they needed was an invitation.

So before you walk out the proverbial door and try to go out and invite people in the highways, byways, bushes, and shrubs, please make sure you have a smile on your face. Please make sure you have an upward inflection. And please, please, *pretty please* make sure that it sounds like good news.

Because this invitation they're receiving is one they actually *need*.

And I'm going to upset what you normally hear from your preachers and turn that invitation upside down: It doesn't have to be an invitation into anybody's church. It might just be an invitation into your home or to a cookout you're doing on Saturday. Maybe they just need to eat and play a board game around you. Maybe they just need to see you act right at a restaurant or in the laundromat.

Any invitation into the presence of a believer in Jesus Christ— and therefore the presence of God because you carry His presence with you—is an invitation worth giving and an invitation worth receiving.

You're on assignment. And that's important because you're supposed to reach a lot of people. People that agree with you and people that don't agree with you. People that believe in you and people that don't believe in you. People who believe what you believe and people who have no idea *what* to believe. It's for everyone.

Don't be afraid of someone rejecting the invitation.

Your assignment is not to drag them there. It's to invite them there.

Do you know the old adage about the odds of a salesman? Knock on fifty doors, and someone will let you in. Knock on one door and you'll be convinced no one will let you in.

Any invitation into the presence of a believer in Jesus Christ—and therefore the presence of God because you carry His presence with you—is an invitation worth giving and an invitation worth receiving.

So ask, seek, and knock. I guarantee you that someone is going to open the door because that someone has actually been waiting for the invitation. You just don't know who it is yet, which is why He said, "Invite everybody." He knows the odds exponentially go up when you invite everybody and not just somebody.

SCRIPTURES FOR FURTHER READING

Here are all the scriptures we dove into throughout this book, in the order we addressed them (minus repeats from subsequent chapters). Take them into your quiet time with the Lord and ask God what He wants to say to you about His words. Look them up and write them down. Post them around your house so you can see them often. Like we talked about—you *can* hear the voice of the Holy Spirit. All you have to do is get to know Him.

Chapter 2
Acts 17:1–9

Chapter 3
John 3:16
Ephesians 1:4–5
Romans 8:28–30

Chapter 4
Romans 5:6–8

Chapter 5
Jeremiah 29:11
Ephesians 2:10
Psalm 18:32
Psalm 139:14
Romans 8:37–39
1 Corinthians 3:16
2 Corinthians 5:12
2 Corinthians 5:20

1 Thessalonians 1:4
2 Timothy 1:7
1 John 3:1

Chapter 6
Matthew 23:1–36

Chapter 7
Acts 19:13–22
Philippians 2:3–11
Deuteronomy 11:18

Chapter 8
Matthew 11:28–30
Romans 10:9

Chapter 9
Amos 5:18–27
Matthew 5:17–20
Isaiah 1:2–20

Chapter 11
Ephesians 6:23–24

Chapter 12
Matthew 5:43–48

Chapter 13
Ephesians 5:18
Romans 8:11

Chapter 14
Acts 10:38

John 14:15–18
John 2:1–11
Matthew 14:13–21
Mark 6:32–44
Luke 9:10–17
John 6:1–14
Luke 19:1–10

Chapter 15
Ephesians 5:2
Nehemiah 8:10

Chapter 16
Matthew 7:3

Chapter 17
John 4:1–30

Chapter 18
Matthew 8:14–15

Chapter 19
Leviticus 24:19–21

Chapter 20
Matthew 22:1–14
Luke 14:15–24
Genesis 3:11

Chapter 21
Luke 23:33–46
Philippians 2:5–8

NOTES

Chapter 3: Spoiler Alert

1. *The Oxford Pocket Dictionary of Current English*, s.v. "predestination," Encyclopedia.com, accessed September 8, 2023, https://www.encyclopedia.com/philosophy-and-religion/christianity /protestant-christianity/predestination.

Chapter 4: Off of a Maybe

1. "I Would Die 4 U," Spotify, track 7 on Prince and the Revolution, *Purple Rain*, NPG Records Inc., under exclusive license to Warner Records Inc., 1984, https://open.spotify.com/album /7nXJ5k4XgRj5OLg9m8V3zc.

Chapter 8: The Sound of It

1. *NLT Study Bible* (Carol Springs, IL: Tyndale, 2017), commentary on Matthew 23:15, emphasis added.

ABOUT THE AUTHOR

Tim Ross gave his life to Jesus on January 14, 1996, and preached his first sermon on February 25, 1996. For nearly thirty years he has preached around the world and served the local church. He now spends his time as a podcaster, influencer, author, consultant, and speaker.

Tim has been married to Juliette since 1999, and they have two sons, Nathan and Noah.

COMPANION BIBLE STUDY
FOR YOUR CHURCH AND SMALL GROUP

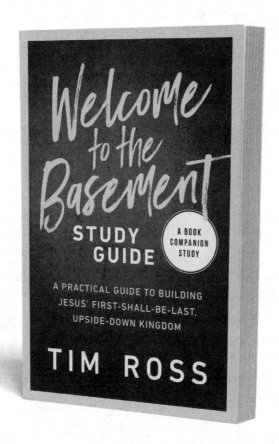

AVAILABLE WHEREVER BOOKS ARE SOLD.